CHAPTER 2

ONE REAL KISS FROM BROTHER PRINCE

CHAPTER 2

ONE REAL KISS FROM BROTHER PRINCE

By Noble Lee Lester

34,099 words

7033 Cavalier Rd

Jacksonville, FL

(904) 895-0162

nobleomagie@hotmail.com

Dedication

To my own girls:
Tara Gray
Nikki Parrish
Rachel Jovita Christina Dawson
Nabila Lee Lester
Bianca Isabel Lester
(Daughter in law: Shayla Ray)
(My grands: Amanda & Lauryn)
(My sister: Cora Lee Turner)
(My mothers: Blanche Raymond & Seanna
Sally Lester) and my loving wife: Lena
Annette Lester
Jesus, The Christ
who continues to teach us all how to
Love like a Brother Prince could.

Warning and Foreword but from the author:

The first thing the "brother" has to do about healing the pain-stricken sister that she might again find faith, hope and security in him is to bury the culture driven fantasy, "Pimp." Live not in her crib but build her a home. Refer to her as a queen and not "momma."

Pimpin' dem bitches and f**kin' dem hoes is NOT what her body, mind and existence is made for. Don't knock the paint off it but paint it with the glorious colors of love and affection.

Yes, we cum in her loins but from there is a portal from the universe whereby comes anything from a Muhammad Ali or a Jesus. Well, maybe not Jesus. (Perhaps "Heysus."

That heavenly portal gate is to be respected. And know this my brother-prince, your love is the keeper of God's gate.

Contents

POEM

LET ME KISS AWAY YOUR SHELL

ONE REAL KISS FROM BROTHER PRINCE

LET'S KISS AWAY THE SPELL

THAT'S TOOK AWAY YOUR EGYPTIAN QUEENDOM EVER

SINCE

LET ME KISS AWAY THE SPELL THAT HANGS HEAVY

OVER YOU.

THAT DARKENS CLOUD OF 2ND CLASS FEELINGS AND

MORNING TEARFUL DEW.

THOSE FEARFUL WALLS THAT PRISON YOU IN AND ME

OUT

THAT MAKE THE WORDS, "I LOVE YOU",

SUSPICIOUS--AND WITH A DOUBT.

LET ME KISS AWAY YOUR SHELL

WITH FRESH NEW SOIL,

KISS AWAY THE SPELL, MY LADY

WITH THY ANOINTING TOIL,

KISS AWAY THE SPELL

WITH MY FERTILE LIFE-GIVING WATERS,

KISS AWAY YOUR GUARDED SHELL

AND LET OUR "LOVE SEEDS" JUST GROW ALL OVER.

With A SMILE

PLEASE, LET BROTHER PRINCE KISS AWAY THE

SPELL.

DELUSIONS OF THEIR OWN GRANDEUR

Beauty is a seed no one can wholeheartedly implant in me. Unlike mother earth where all elements come together to spawn any seedling, it only lies dormant inside me—the GMO has no metaphoric place here. Only I can assure the plant-germ of anything DNA in myself effectively. My visions, passions, dreams, drives and desires are only ideas only I can fertilize with a self-appointed feeling of worth that I discover.

Now, all that might be easy to say. But to engage myself with such confidence is another thing all together.

Friendly compliments can certainly help my drives and desires, but at the end of the day, my growth is all mines to believe in and nourish. A good friend, a parent or a wonderful mate cannot be solely responsible for my inner growth and wellbeing—so many might believe. My courage cannot be the responsibility of any coach.

WHO CAN SUGGEST I HAVE COURAGE?

A lover can perhaps assist me or even inspire me with such. Friends can support our decisions but that's only limited to their established beliefs in themselves, their own feelings of worth. Their helping-hand can only be the extent of their human commitment and that can be a full-time job unto itself handling their own business and emotional baggage.

For so many years, I fell short and disarm my own powers by allowing myself to believe that "others" had the power to empower me. I reflect on ex-lovers and wives:

…If only you'd trust me Judy; gave me more time Bettye; saw the vision Ruby; put the abortion off Lisa; heard my lyrics Tracey; not played me Estina; let me help you Penny, I would have been a contender and made it—made something great of myself.

My opinion, but I think Jesus or God wants us to initiate that cause, the cause of self-esteem. With unattainable standards I placed on others, I tend to think the same of others that I too had the power to empower them or control them. None of which, I discovered, I was capable of, or did effectively.

With this thinking, of someone empowering me, I subjected myself to looking for the

"perfect-mate" or "perfect-lover" I thought
that power was physically represented by
aesthetic beauty. I would look for these
qualities in a candidate-partner I'd meet.
Obviously, I would reject those that showed
so-called "imperfections." I also subjected
myself to look for constant approval from
these "perfectly" assessed and selected gems.
Ironically, I would wonder often why there
were always so far and few in between—these
"perfect-people." Why did the "real-them"
always come out later and "show their ass"
(bad side) later? I was so befuddled by their
snobbish, bourgeois-behavior. I mean, after
all, they started out perfect. I foolishly
thought beautiful people were wholly good,
willed people.

"Where is that "perfect person" I fell in love with?!"

I suspect strongly I was emotionally
immature, or wisdom deprived. I never stopped
to realize if someone, other than me, was my
only source of inner inspiration. I looked to
the cool ones, the hip-ones and the "perfect-
people" to encourage me—define me via their
populous in-crowd trending.

- What happens when the "cool-ones" are no
  longer around. I never considered that?

Separation, break-ups, divorce, death, etc.

- What then?
- Will my world end or shatter?

High expectations or standard needed from others is simply non-existent and un-lasting when and if ever we stumbled upon them.

Perfection in a relationship is time spend together, I realized. I began to figure that true love came with the ups and downs. "Time served" (LOL) together, not in the imprisoned sense, but sticking-together and learning each other's ways and learning to accept each other more importantly. This took perfect time.

My partner can only influence my own nurtured self-worth. They can only endorse that which I have learned and decided upon. As I stumble along, in error, trying to make my way, I realized my partner can only accept, support, love and adore my friendship—or not. After all, acceptance is a form of love.

We will all physically change with time. Therefore, any expressions of beauty between us will alter as we grow older. "You look marvelous," "You are so stunning," "Wow, so handsome" and even that is limited in the solidarity of love, acceptance and the time spent. It is in time; love becomes the value of something else other than beauty.

But still, these are wonderful complements to share with a significant other—anyone would love to hear them. But as we grow, it is not the sole sustainer for longevity in a love union. This is where "I" (self) comes in to take over and learn to love all the changes with time.

Again, our partners are only a support unit subject to their own limitations which is always short of "perfect." Sure, partners can temporarily excite us with good feelings, assist with our sexual satisfaction and beauty-glow. Couples can even plant affection that influence our sense of peace, joy and happiness but never our self-esteem or sense of worth and confidence.

Our inner "love-seeds," i.e., kindness, compliments, kudos to the man-in-the-mirror, is an effective human *Miracle Gro* that makes our day and puts a fertilized bounce in our step. But, true worth, appreciation and self-love start with liking yourself. It is what Noble Lee, you, them and they think of our self. My loving spouse, my partner and my friend cannot fix me—only really secure me—"I'm here." This is a connection I make with me, God or the universe.

Friendship encouragement can be a mighty jump-start. It launches the spirit to want better, or more of, to desire finer qualities and to grow further. Appreciation is a wonderful booster too for "talking someone off the ledge." But ultimately, appreciation is left up to me to decide how it'll steep down in my soul and take effect in my heart.

Extending gratitude and thanks to family for kindness they have offered and what they have graciously done can be a powerful means of influencing ongoing friendship. No doubt, this will initiate added good to whatever the friend, or family, member brings to the relationship; provided it's genuinely supportive and positive. It will always result in being creditable and a "love-seed."

Stable relationships require so much of the above—it's hard work. In order to adjust and then accept each other with trust, respect and appreciation, we require these above "love-seeds" exercised. Excuse me for sounding corny, but it's like feeding nested chicks who grope for more—they are spiritually fatten by the efforts of momma--fowl's love. We must feed each other love, and at the same time, train each other to return the "feeding" as a culture. "...*Thou shall love thy neighbor as thy self.*"[1]

Again, it's a real job being a friend, a spouse, a lover or a partner. These "seeds" will grow stronger and sweeter as we learn from each other in time with mutual exchange of kindness. During this time of getting to know each other, we accept our differences, and they you.

Especially the uncomfortable and un-favored similarities, they're the "human-faults" we don't like so much. Listening to criticism is painful. Those are the feelings we work through in each other that yield emotional rewards and provoke lasting solidarity.

Each gender, or family member, brings something challenging and new to the relationship and sometimes that challenge can be trying. Before the gems of happiness reveal them self, groundwork of mutual give and take must come into visible play.

I like to call these challenges "life exams." Living with others is a test but living with your self is an exam.

The love support game where we cope with behavioral challenges, anomalies, and different lifestyles without the necessity of

---

[1] Matt: 22:39 King James Version

personal perfection is game we don't want to play:

"Lord I wish "they" would do this or that, or could "they" be more like them…"

…this a personal test where nothing is perfect, but everything is perfectly complied to be imperfectly perfect? In other words, you're gonna screw this up.
It's the trouble that many racists get into wanting someone so-called "odd" to their circle to be the "perfect them" meeting up with their perfect approval—how can that be? It ain't gonna happen. The "odd" one will probably think the same of the racist; wanting them or wishing them to change as well. The ONLY thing we can change are our thoughts. However, is there any truth to a prince's transforming kiss?
Shall we read on?

#

VALENTINE CARDS ARE NOT JUST FOR GIRLS

Researchers have found and proven that men and women share similar ideas on romance and love. Men are just as romantic as women. But some choose to think that the women capitalize on the idea. Men might approach it in different ways, expressions and manners are different, but both want and need the same kind of comfort, appreciation, and feeling of affection from each other, and I venture to trust that nothing makes us stronger, really. The general romantic tendency for men is the "seasonal" romance. You know, the challenge of wooing (pick-up lines), the courtship (The pursuant), the conquering (Getting to third base). Battling his approach fears, having to force himself to move into her bubble and bust-make-a-move. You know, "come-on lines" or make a play and order her a drink. It's age-old stuff—rituals. Most men like the thrill of finding the perfect charm-filled words to get to "first base" and "around" triumphantly; building her confidence about the idea of "them" all at the same time. This is what some men like--the feeling that they've achieved, won, or conquered someone.

Then, like many men, once the "championship ring" is gotten (so he thinks) the ritual of romance begin to fade or is no longer in the forefront of his thinking--remember the game is over. "I got the trophy on my shelf" --forever! She's wearing the ring!

Whereas with her, if she approves of his courtship and "come on" tactics, the romance is the overture to the impending grand opera. Now, the show can begin. Or better, it's the music in the lobby as she rushes to her seat and awaiting the curtain to open. It's the overture, baby! She wants to move now into Act I exposition.

Romance is equally "general" for the woman. But however, in my streetwise opinion, it must be ongoing, a reaffirming commitment and traditional repeated mantras of reoccurring expressions of romantic dating. There is a real need for her to be wanted, needed, as well as respected and appreciated with regularity.

These romantic needs aren't insecurities, as many men often mistake them for, but real love fuel (The glue of affection). It's love fuel that secures commitment. This is vital to the spiritual health and daily survival of the relationship.

These thoughts are very often regarded by some men as over-indulgence, overly emotional, high maintenance or "needy"; far from it, sirs. It is the very lifeline of the relationship survival and success. She is fueled by warmth, smiles of happiness and affection. When this is done with regularity, her spirit attaches itself to the man and cuddling becomes a symbol of that bond. From this union onward, she begins to finish his thoughts, anticipates his reactions, and sometimes actually feels **his** own emotions that have not surfaced in him.

Love is vital to nourishment for peace, stress less and better living environments. Love is a study guide in a world filled with "life exams" (challenges). Love is spiritual food we all feed from; like animals, who once finds trust in a human and bonds with them, starve for their human-friend's affections.

Pediatricians and child theorist solidly agree, across the board, that a premature baby, once life support and nourishment is administered, balances between life and death most often by warmth, touch and emanating love of the parents or guardian. The parent's love and grace are its fate when life hangs in the balance. Love is difference between life and death with infants. It is love and grace that is the true spiritual "umbilical cord" that connects human life with the source of the universe's force to live. And I believe this force is "God."

Love is that conduit that force; an invisible, sustaining, ever-present, ever needed force that is desperately fundamental. It's a human need that is a cure-all. There is NO snake oil, root-spell, or elixir like love.

Some say, "God is love" and there lay our intrinsic will to live, to ascertain more of it. If not, we are sorely disappointed. I agree wholeheartedly. We survive solely because of it. And, by the hand of this great power, we are commissioned to share it equally, spread it far and wide--I don't mean sex that's another book, chapter, and verse ("Don't fig leaf out," Bouquet #7) but affection and kindness is the AED (heart start defibrillator) for courtship.

"Love don't love nobody"—so sang The Spinners, a Motown singing group from the 1970's. They were simply lamenting that love is about the business of love. The more love we are opened to, the more we grow in it, and it strives in us. When we are willing to share our love, we are more susceptible to being loved aplenty. It is the definition of Eastern

Indian philosophy of cornucopia: the source of abundance.

In 1974, I was introduced to Kahil Gibran's "The Phophet," 1923, "Love" (the poem):

"...When you love you should not say, "God is in my heart," but rather, "I am in the heart of God."
And think not you can direct the course of love, for love, if it finds you worthy, directs your course."

In 1973, I was also introduced to Ken Keyes, Handbook to Higher Consciousness, 1972. These are the stages of our consciousness that we must grow from and to find our self in the heart of God's love:

#

[2]THE SEVEN CENTRES OF CONSCIOUSNESS

1. THE SECURITY CENTER

This Center makes you preoccupied with food, shelter, money or whatever you equate with your personal security. This programming forces your consciousness to be **dominated by your continuous battle to get "enough"** from the world in order to feel secure.

2. THE SENSATION CENTER

This Center is concerned with finding happiness in life by providing yourself with more and better pleasurable sensations and activities. **For many people, sex is the most appealing of all sensations: drugs, sugar, carbohydrates.** Other addictive sensations may include the sound of music, the taste of food, etc.

3. THE POWER CENTER

When your consciousness is focused on this Center, you are concerned with **dominating people and situations and increasing your prestige, wealth, and pride -- in addition to thousands of more subtle forms of hierarchy, manipulation, politics, propaganda and control.**

4. **THE LOVE CENTER**

At this Center you are transcending subject-object relationships and are learning to see the world with the feelings and harmonies of flowing acceptance. You see yourself in everyone and everyone in yourself. You feel compassion for the suffering of those caught in the dramas of security, sensation, and power centers. You are beginning to love and accept everyone unconditionally -- even yourself more importantly.

5. THE CORNUCOPIA CENTER

When your consciousness is illuminated by this Center, you experience the friendliness of the **world you are creating.** You begin to realize that you've always lived in a perfect world. To the degree that you still have addictions, the perfection lies in giving you the experience you need to get free of your emotion-backed demands. As you reprogram your addictions, the perfection will be experienced as a continuous enjoyment of the here and now in your life. As you become more loving and accepting, the world becomes a "horn of plenty" that gives you more than you need to be happy.

---

[2] Extraction: "Handbook to higher consciousness," by Ken Keys, Jr., 1972

6. THE CONSCIOUS-AWARENESS CENTER

It is liberating to have a Center from which your Conscious awareness watches your body and mind perform on the lower five centers. This is a meta-center from which you non-judgmentally witness the drama of your body and mind. From this Center of Centers, you learn to impartially observe your social roles and life games from a place that is **free from fear and vulnerability.**

7. THE COSMIC CONSCIOUSNESS CENTER

When you live fully in the Sixth Center of Consciousness, you are ready to transcend self-awareness and become pure awareness. At this ultimate level, you are **one with everything -- you are love, peace, energy, beauty, wisdom, clarity, effectiveness, and oneness.**

The evidence is clear. Love expects us to continually to plant the seed of love in each other and more importantly our self.

This perhaps might be a misconception among Christians who feel the passionate need to help SAVE others for a promising kingdom in the afterlife. Maybe SAVE might also suggest, in metaphor, that we LOVE each other to fortify a kingdom of good right here on Earth. Maybe heaven isn't an after effect but a near and now reality.

We are reminded by this need to love by praising each other as well as God, caring, listening, understanding, being there, saluting, sharing and moreover accepting one another with constancy.

Our holidays and our recognized celebrated novelty days exist to foster the economy, or hustle our wallets, yes. But it also facilitates our need for love. For example (e.g.), Valentine Day, Mother's Day, Secretary's Day, Father's Day, birthday celebrations, Black History month and Memorial Day, etc., all designed to express some affection. Sure, they are designed to stimulate national economics but again they are also designed to express love and thanks originally; designed for gentle excuses to exchange and permeate loved.

The Canadians celebrate along with us and yet even more, e.g., Victoria Day, St-Jean, Canada Day, Remembrance Day and Boxing Day…? Even fighters gain some salutation of affection through recognition.

Some fundamentally and passionately believe that God loves love also. He/she/"it" is loved by praise especially.

> "… *Let the peoples praise you, O God;*
> *let all the peoples praise you!*
> *The earth has yielded its increase;*
> *God, our God, shall bless us…"* Psalm 67

Hebrews 13:15 By him therefore let us offer the sacrifice of praise to God continually, that is, the fruit of our lips giving thanks to his name.

1 Peter 2:9 But you are a chosen generation, a royal priesthood, an holy nation, a peculiar people; that you should show forth the praises of him who has called you out of darkness into his marvellous light;

Revelation 7:12 Saying, Amen: Blessing, and glory, and wisdom, and thanksgiving, and honour, and power, and might, be to our God for ever and ever. Amen.[3]

We praise "The Lord Jesus," "God," "Allah," "Yahweh," or whatever our "Universal Intelligence" choice might be. We praise "its" holy name." They require love as well; deities and humans alike need LOVE. Like god, we all require simple praise like:

■■

"Hello," "How do you do?" "Let me open that for you." "Oh, that's okay." "You're fine." "OR, a drive-by smile and hand wave…

The simpler the regard for love the sweeter we find life to be "cornucopia."

Love is a constant ever turning law of the universe. Love is hospitality—"The customer is always right" is a hospitable regard and respect for the client.

It's no wonder that so many religious entities celebrate and praise God with: Ash

---

[3] http://www.godvine.com/bible/category/praise
Bible Gateway

Wednesday, Palm Sunday, Good Friday, and
Easter Sunday, Passover, Rosh Hashanah, Yom
Kippur, Thanksgiving, Hanukah, Kwanzaa and
Jesus' birthday, i.e., Christmas. It's clear
God ("it") likes to be appreciated. For me,
during Christmas, I can feel gladness in the
air.

■■

Psalm 100 King James Version (KJV)

*Make a joyful noise unto the LORD, all ye
lands.*

*2 Serve the LORD with gladness: come before his
presence with singing.*

*3 Know ye that the LORD he is God: it is he that
hath made us, and not we ourselves; we are his
people, and the sheep of his pasture.*

*4 Enter into his gates with thanksgiving, and
into his courts with praise: be thankful unto
him and bless his name.*

*5 For the LORD is good; his mercy is
everlasting; and his truth endureth to all
generations.*

WHEN SUSANNA JONES WEARS RED!!

Now, how do we infuse this healing love into "The Bouquet Race"?

Surely, we can agree that African Americans need a hug; some "mirror-mirror on the wall" who tells us: "I accept you, I love you, I appreciate you, I believe in you, you are awesome, and you are wonderful most of all."

How do we turn "ghettos" into communal homes of good living that emanate less doom and gloom but sunshine and Jasmine bloom?

How does one love their own race, culture, and social traditions after such extended political and inhumane damage?

1939 to 1945 the European Jews met hell's gateway and thereafter their Exodus to these United States where they found more hatred because of religious differences. And they lamented for decades in America by the hand of discrimination, terrorism, and vandalism with no good reason. Yet, the African, for 400 years, has no sympathy or empathy for his swelling anger. The best this country can do for him is incarcerate him: "Orange is his new Black"?

Without celebrated credit his blues has been taken: Jazz? Do-Wop? Dance? High spirits? Killed his community leaders? Use his woman? Stole his soul-food recipes and called them "Southern-Cuisine? Exploited his physical sportsman powers? Imitated his Barry White's voice? His Motown sounds.

Without a doubt, I love Jewish celebrations like: Kosher weddings and Bar Mitzvahs; Greek plate smashing at weddings or to mourn their loss; the Mardi Gra; Indian bling wedding; the Brooklyn Caribbean parade as well as I adored the idea of my brother Spencer Lester jumping the broom to celebrate his wedding vows. I love ancient ruins and all the mythological tales.

I am in awe of French performing arts—Cirque du Soleil; The Roman Cathedral-Vatican City takes my breath away. German auto-technology, I long to drive fast; The Swedish tax systems and health care is a dream. Canadian comics make me howl with laughter. The Indian Bollywood musicals blow my mind. Asian herbs and their holistic medicines and teas I can't learn enough of. El Paca and Llama furs are beyond minks to my skin. Brazilian fusion jazz is amazing. The Pigmy rain forest and Chile Mountains are simply unbelievable. You name it and can find love in

other traditions and ethnicities. What would
the world be like without it? What's not to
love?

As well, I chose to adore what I've come
to be, an African as well as all God's other
wonders I've listed above.

I also love Brown women madly. I have 5
daughters of my own:

Tara, Nikki, Rachael Jovita, Nabila and Bianca. And now, grandchildren: Amanda and Lauryn

I love *watching* all women. They're like
flowers, live sculptures of fine arts or
masterful paintings; a kaleidoscopic beauty to
me; they exist wonderfully. I especially like
watching them walk, the way some strut and the
best part is watching them walk away observing
all the incredible moving parts like an
asymmetrical machine; her curves that charm my
soul and lures my libido to spark; in the
infamous words of the 1960's songwriter Roy
Iverson, who could not have said it simpler,
"Mercy!" What a joy it is to witness such
lucid creatures—as if in slow motion—like a
Venus apparition floating feather light on a
breeze. Then there is that moment of delay;
the anticipated hint of perfume as she passes
by… Ahhh, yes…! Then, you prepare yourself

visually for the main event, the grand finale', watching that "badonkadonk" rump trunk decrescendo as she struts on and from afar. All the while, shifting her impervious motions with a rhythm seemingly in sync to an inner universal tempo with mother earth herself—"Sweet silver trumpets, Jesus when Susanna Jones wears red…" (Langston Hughes).

The woman is a phenomenon that pronounces something profoundly mysterious yet is delicately logical. All the "wild" my total attention is being caressed by her natural outline, like a glimmering perfect rare chocolate diamond.

No, I am not a stalker, but I'm certain most women are aware but those who don't know there is a depth of visual pleasure they bring to men simply being themselves. Sometimes that is all that is necessary to please us men.

Rufus Thomas sang it most appropriately, "Shake it, don't you break it, wrap it up and I'll take it!" "It must be jelly 'cause jam don't shake like that!" ("Chummy" Macgregor, 1940's) "Good googa-mooga!" (Jimmy and the teenchordials, 1950's). All these cool cat men are gone but the power of their indescribable affections vividly echoes on in their maleness and passions for the woman.

Don't get me wrong. I enjoy the human-
garden and the smell of all the sapien-flowers
in the fields of life but I'm less inclined to
pick or pot such fine art to which I distantly
observe. However, I do appreciate them, only.
I am, however, of a monogamous mind to plant
only one and that is my own dear bride, Queen
and better half…

Lena Annette Lester.

I monogamously sunshine, fertilize, water
and germinate her; my ONE soulmate as often as
I can—or age allows--LOL. Because our
commitment is the true beauty that means
everything to us, and we know it is life
giving and love sustaining—committed love. Our
love-seeds are many things, but faithfulness
and trust are our key.

Let your fountain be bless, and rejoice

With the wife of your youth.

As loving deer and a grateful doe, let
her
Breast satisfy you at all times; and
always be
Enraptured with her love.
(Proverbs 5:18-19)

Amen?

#

DAMSEL IN DURESS

It is my sincerest prayer, as a nation, we all racially and collectively come to know inner joy, self-esteem, and self-worth that we might clamor to cheeringly endorse "self-value" in each other—of all races. The Star-Ship Enterprise is still trying to give us a hint. Intergalactic beings are Gene Roddenberry's idea of diversification.

Brown women have had the burden of solidifying all the above—all races. Yes, she has been our lonely workhorse from central casting trying to get us to get along. She's always taken the lead here and with little help. She's allowed the Indian families to hide in our African-DNA, side by side battles with the Irish in Hell's Kitchens, cop-beats and boxing rings, supported the discriminated Jewish commerce and Gouda-cheese and thin sliced bologna, we turn our heads and held our snitches from Italian Mafia numbers-runners, we hauled goods and purchased prohibition white-trash distillery products (Blue & moonshine) and danced madly in the speak-easy Cottons Clubs of Harlem for the Hebrew-gangsters and Murder, Inc. She's done her part. By our help, will she continue to pass down these wonderful traits among our forthcoming generations of offspring? You dam right because that's how she rolls. However, have we given up on her?

Well, there's another "Talk-Show."

Nationalism is about mom. It is by her our children will learn about everyone and everything. From the woman's breath, breast, attitude, and actions, they will learn the work of self-love, self-acceptance and self-appreciation and the love of the Lord.

She will teach them how to redeem our 400 years of "love lost." She'll teach them that although there is a storm behind us with not much reparation in view, there is still hope in holding up each other, supporting one another and to "git yo' lesson." -Seanna Lester

Sure, we've lost a great deal of inner power. Hell, Jim-Crow is a blow to anyone. Far too many Brown women have had to put up with traveling the corridors of the ghetto-bitten, deprived reddened, turned away and thrown back "unforgiving" environments.

The Willie Lynch stories, whether they're fictitious or true, have the Negro women and her children forced to observe their own lynched. Even if "Willie" is a metaphor, they systematically forced to observe such cultural spectacle. Any penalty of the African male's so-called criminal's doings like "Black-Lives-Matter" peaceful-protest after being video'd shot in the street is an observed "Willie-ism." Black men have suffered imprisonment by asking to purchase property, inquiring about voting, looking at a white woman or a horse inadvertently, hitting a white man back defensively, not moving off a sidewalk where whites tread. This can and has caused many to lose a lot of confidence and love in White people and unfortunately themselves.

What's a woman to do?

Should she not fear the jeopardy of her child's livelihood?

Should she resist and not be forced by any white man's bidding?

This conditioning has been based on her training to coexist among white society and racist demons. The exercise of securing the life of her children has been not of creativity but caution: Do's and Don'ts when talking to a "cracker." She done what she's had to do; turn their eyes of pride away from self-respect and submit to his crazed and oppressive ways for survival. Racism is the cause of "Zombism" in America and we need an anecdote.

These practices of slavery and such may have happened many years ago, but the principals are still etched in our base of thinking—like the confederacy monuments. Again, women still cautiously train their children to co-behave amid white authorities: "Let them crackers vote in who they want!" "Keep your head down." "They control the purse strings child!"

"You know they gon redline blacks out of neighborhoods and re-zone them schools' districts."

"Let them, they're going to re-set the laws anyway; re-set educational standards and put us "criminals" away for decades for smoking a damn joint, and now they are selling billion-dollar joints legally."

"But I'll be damned if you gonna git away with shooting my kids!!" These are the untold stories spoken freely and non-publicly on Black porches across the country during the '50's, 60's and '70's.

Equally, many whites are thrown by excessive "street-sentencing" when Blacks "step out of line" and the consequences are the 2014 & 2015 police shootings and deaths of young and older Black men--that's excessive behavior for out-of-line infractions. Or worse, the disrespect of our 45th president, these discrediting attacks were out of line.

This brainwashing and social conditioning must come to an end for the sake of our nation, women, guardianship, mental health, and management of our children. We are making them and ourselves crazy with resentment and lack of trust.

Black women too are children of the universe, our God, trying, just as Black men, to recover from the atrocities of emotional challenges, social color wars and political blights and social absenteeism. These women are not waylaid victims of humanity. They've paid in full their place in this society. Reparation now is not the cash they grope after but the assumed dignity. "Open the door, I'll get it myself." --James Brown.

There are many who are still lost or left in the slums waiting to be rescued, saved, retrieved away from the stronghold and grip of the lessening esteem-demons called discrimination. Too many have succumbed, adapted, and adjusted to it as a natural way of life, unchallenged and with parasite-like existence.

We must seriously prepare for a behavioral reform to eradicate bottom feeding addictions: drug infestation, non-certifiable employment, domestic abuse, flesh work, ill-educated discredited non-redeemable degrees and glass ceiling careers, excessive alcohol usage and less than dignified exploitative clothing and apparel all of which is a result of prolonged oppression. I am not blaming but oppressive pressure like slavery in America requires therapy. The Bouquet Race is broken. This is a rescue-mission. It is a live or die "life exam" that cannot fail, and it can't be handled by herself, the Black woman alone. She needs Brother Prince's assumed assistance.

These afflictions will beget and reproduce other lesser modes of existence and the cycle of craziness will repeat for generations to come. Generations of black men are filling the prisons and 13th Amendment is having its unintended way. Therefore, we must seize fast and summon our children's self-likeability (love) with the patience of Job to reform self-perception— "I am-Somebody." To which we are."[4]

When assisting her, we must interject the idea of hopeful change in her heart. We need a therapeutic social clinic at the workplace, in the homes, at the church and on the streets of readied caretakers to help. Perhaps a requirement of all churches where young women

---

[4] William Holmes Borders, poem: 1950 (popularized by Jesse Jackson)

are tutored on life-saving issues like health,
child-rearing, teacher-parent communication
and co-work, sexuality, contraception, mental
and emotion health, menopause preparation all
administered by older, elder, wise, and mature
church mothers. Perhaps it can be called,
"Mother." Call it what you want: just do
something.

There, a needful lady could seek guidance
with the help of experienced eyes to assist
her with decisions upon a chosen make-over and
self-acceptance. To many times, we thrown our
hands up with hopeless and retired with "It is
what it is." "They're far gone and
irreversible." "They don't want to do better
to pull themselves up." It took roughly 400
years to set this madness to motion. With a
small chisel and much patience, this is our
required duty to chip away until we get out of
this pillar-of-salt harden state.

Okay, okay!! I feel your resistance, your
fear of getting involved and risking
disappointment. I get it. You've tried before.
I get your apprehension. Granted, some cannot
be helped beyond the scars of depravation,
long suffering, and bottom feeding. Sometimes
the damage is so done, so ingrain, for so
long, in their souls that it's terminal,
inoperable and seemingly no-use.

But what choice do we have for our children? How much is too much, too long, for them? If we don't move, they will continue to roam the streets finding more and more hell to fertilize their begotten no good. Evil is real and evil devours.

All this can be redirected. When she, or we, break through, let us proactively prepare to receive her wounded hearts with an open mind. Let us be ready to assist them as much as they would allow us and rebuild a soul that never had a chance. It only takes one step at a time with consistency.

Angry threatening inner-city behavior can turn peaceful, loving or family oriented. Sure, expect doubt, suspicion, and creepy behavior what else have they've learned? We must help those with their lack of focus, aimless preoccupations, and broken spirits of hope—it's what was taught, and they took the white-instructions well. People must be taught to visualize, dream pragmatically and plan systematically. I'm no expert, or motivation speaker Les Brown, but perhaps start with asking comfortable fewer condescending questions, with a hospitable tone:

What's up? What are you doing?

You enjoy it? Sounds like it.

What do you want to do with it—you think?

Who else you admire does it?

You think you could do it differently?

If you had everything or everybody you needed, where would you start first?

If you had people to help you, what would you have them do first?

How would this help others?

What would you like to profit by it?

You sound like you're good at this. Are you?

This sort of gentle questions is a matter of courage that we might speak a word of encouragement. We must be not so preoccupied with our own apprehension but look for the signs of joy in their eyes and follow those leads down their rabbit hole.[5]

What can I do with the unknown? I don't know them.

Well, you can expand yourself by listening to something different out of the box that isn't your own routine. That's what your questions are asking of the person or interviewee. You're asking them to explore an unknown.

There is no manual for the right questions but there is nothing like sincerity when building a rapport. Keep it 100 and be for-real. And there's nothing like fear to run

---

[5] Alice in Wonderland (take chances with the unknown)

others and yourself away, but courage cuts through everything if you're willing and real.

We have an inner voice that guides us. To put one's religion out there is never the point, but heart is always the truth. The "Holy Spirit" is in ALL of us; pray and mediate, it will guide you to be for real. We don't always know what to do or say and that's what's scary. But the "spirit" does know.

I know Yoda[6] is a cartoon but the writer George Lucas felt the need to share his philosophical belief: The "Force" flows through us all and it is indeed a great power by righteousness. Equally, there are evil forces that serve us failingly and to our demise.

I promise you it WILL be revealed to you when you step out with courage. Provided that you *decide* an answer will be rendered to you— the trick is not to doubt. Remember the ying and yang, good or bad, right, or wrong is ever ready to be engaged by the "Force" by your decisions or choices. The universe, God, "It" works.

Nevertheless however, the same power works if you decide there is *nothing* I can do— nothing will happen. The universe follows you, us. We order our own steps. Yes? God waits for

---

[6] A Star War philosophical puppet character 1974

your order that he might assist fulfilling
your steps.

Being vulnerably foolish during these
stages of help for the wayward, lending a hand
and our assistance is not always help to the
poor at heart or the unfocused. They might
interpret your meekness for weakness. Being
"watchful as a serpent and kind as a dove" is
a way of looking cautiously before you leap
for them. I am not talking about distrust.
Sure, they're going to "play" you. It's what
they know; they know nothing else but the
game. To them, kindness and altruism is phony,
or they've never learned these hospitable
behaviors; only cheating works for them, right
now.

We must be about rebuilding and saving
love by reaching and teaching with the same
verve and passion we have for saving *souls* as
Christians—which are two very different
things; two very different therapies.

Many of these wayward and broken souls
are commonly Christians. They are lost in
their nebulous dismay of themselves. The word
says they should be or feel this or that, but
life contradicts these scriptures, and their
beliefs often leave them with guilt that
they've done something sinful or wrong unto
God's eyes—far from it. After a lifetime of

disappointment, their beliefs and how this religious "thing" does not nor has not work for them give up on the "Holy Spirit" or "The Force" if you will.

As difficult as one could imagine, the effort to reach into the "ghetto" in full awareness that you might "draw back a nub" (lost hand or life) is daunting. It's very scary. But keep in mind the dangerous world we'll all tread in if we do nothing; your neighborhoods, finances, political base, education, and children won't change for the better it will continue to perpetuate as it has.

Cowering away because of possible dangers is no help while they remain in their status quo. We must chase poverty and ignorance like Popeye Doyle chased down the French Connection—to stamp heroine out. And like Popeye, most of the causes for poverty are principalities in high place feeding off the bait of the wayward. It's gotta be done or many poverty-addicted people will die.

What about the hood-bullies?

Don't fear the "ghetto pit-bull" from across the tracks from da' hood. He is only as vicious and threatening as we might imagine he is. It's his defense mechanism against the unrighteous he knows that exploits him. Mostly he's mad and don't know why. The bully knows where drugs come from and that there're dropped on him. He knows the police, judges and prosecutor are in bed with the "drug-dropper." He knows you make him, and his grandma wait extra longer in the ER. He knows you made the meth-head white boy his supervisor…just because. He knows you never pick the real ball-handlers in your NBA draft because you don't know them/him/us—or the Rucker. What you know is he's brown and appears safe. The Pit-Bull fears the helping hand as much as he's hoping we fear him. The bull has learned to fear the indefinable world of human uncertainty. He is riddled with uncertainty. Just as we fear him, he is equally afraid of our altruistic hand-outs which he cannot perceive as sincere welfare. And like any wayward child, given a similar stressful environment, he knows no motive to give back with love and affection. In fact, it shows weakness. He's learned the past has only taught self-defense and to attack the helpless before the shoe drops.

All humans are the same when they are afraid to trust. When they know no love, they cannot share any. It's the result of inner-city depravity. Love will never come out until it's ushered out with self-esteem.

Outreach: this is a MUST. We're only going to pay for it on the back end with lives, valued property, court-cost, state, or county prison taxes. White people will grow to fear them and racist will use them for political prowess. The longer they remain in these hellholes fighting and killing each other over chips, snacks, snicker-bars, eye-balling and so-called territory claiming, the "pit-bull" will only return to us (i.e., society) angrier than before and back on the streets for more social rejection, trumped up fear charges based on policing and legal probationary abuse.

The political rats are playing out their learned behavior also. Many are still angry at their Confederate lost, giving Blacks emancipation, fighting to launch 13th amendment guaranteeing your slavery once incarcerated, setting up scenarios to arrest you or legally shoot you, fooling themselves into believing they had nothing to do with the above list. And now, they fear you're gaining a stronghold on the political scene where they further fear Blacks will avenge the evil they've done.

The "middle-class" to rich run to suburban safe havens where ghetto throwbacks can't afford to dwell. And they politically make sure that property Redlines of demarcation are set in stone behind policed gated communities.

We must find a way to love lost people. It is our duty to heal everyone. White spoilage, greed, and unearned privilege, other than skin color, will never fix either problem. We must love the lost despite themselves. Treat them like "Nell" (Jodie Foster) or the "Thunder Dome" children (Tina Turner) or the "Lost Boys of Sudan." We must love them like we love the Sun's warmth, like we love paid vacations, like we love to have fun coupled with laughter; like we love free picnic food, good church friends; like we love Christmas gifts and families who laugh out loud, adults and children alike. And when we help, remember that change is foreign and unfamiliar. It takes time and patience. Watch them like a trained St. Bernard because they are unbridled, and reform takes courage, wisdom, and tough love as you trudge through the potential avalanche of the misbegotten. Although some will get stormed upon by overwhelming bad weather but there is light at the end of the dark, fumy tunnel where there is love, respect and honor.

#

NORMAL WOMEN...?

Not just Brown women are deserving of kindness, rescuing and love but all women are.

It makes for a better world: "When momma ain't happy…" Yes, nobody is happy. Especially the "normal ones" mothers, hardworking, worshipping, career driven mothers aren't happy.

You know the "normal ones?"

Normal is an uncomfortable word for me but those women type listed above also aren't physically normal shaped like toothpicks, or those who wear a size 2, who look like human clothes hangers, who can't afford breast implants and aren't naturally blond, I mean *those* "normal women." The majority normal women don't fit these descriptions--no matter what color or nationality they are. It's all unreal.

Yet we force them into these validating, approval, and "perfect" molds they cannot live up to; tearing them apart from the inside not being able to live up the these "great expectations." White women run the risk of damaging their hair with blond dyes and bleach, skin cancer from excessive solar exposure, breast and buttock implants eroding, toxic collagen and Botox injections and the latest resurgence: the corset squeeze. "Normal women" trying to be something they were never biologically intended to be.

And black women...?

#

MADISON AVENUES' BLUES

But how does the normal compete with these Madison Avenue female fancy images and expectations?

Let me introduce you to normal: The size 12 and up IS normal! Oh, I am aware of what a lot of women say they want in sizes. But the reality is what?

Dr. Oz did a quantitative study where he found: "The average man likes size 12 and above compared to lower size-fantasies" but most men are afraid, or petrified, to admit such a thing to weight obsessed family members, girlfriends, and wives.

I have heard of divorces resulting in such questions.

So, what about Madison Avenue?

Why do they have to matter so much to us?

We exist in a society where our commercial ideal and sexual fantasy is an emasculate, anorexic type person with "z" cup implants: Made to order golden-streaks of blond dye, weight-watched streamlines coke-bottle mummy-tucked and wrap shapes with Olympic extremities and long legs that hang from the armpits.

How does a real normal woman compete with these unreal Madison Avenue images?

(TV voice-over) "Well my friends your dreams can come true! What, with designer facial surgeons, Dr. Titsmore Silicone, all insurance accepted wonder policies? If you ACT NOW: go in today a real "normal woman" and after 6 months of recovery from pain and public shame, and FaceBook comments that ask, "Girl, what happen to your face?!" not to leave out non-medical insurance coverage and a ¼ of a million-dollar deduction fee. You'll exit the doctor's office looking like Madam Venus Leather-Face. You can get a whole new look! If you call now, we'll throw in a double-A on the go go go vibrator!! It's a limited offer. Call now!!" Yeah, right!

The key word here is **fee**. What do ya' do when your insurance policies don't quite cover these costs? When the insurance company gets real with the "real woman" and rejects her procedure as a "luxury item," what's a "Cover Girl" to do? Like most of us, we pay our monthly premiums on time for years…!

Everyone doesn't earn the wages and income that afford such premium full-coverage medical policies; even the normal upper middle-class American white woman suffers here.

So, what does the "normal" Venus-hungry need to feel beautiful woman get? Well, like most, she gets an "affordable" medical plus dental discount coupon plan for $19 per month where but a few grouped physicians and dentists honor a 20% deduction for small procedures and mail-order 30-day bulk generic meds—from god knows where. And now, ACA (ObamaCare) isn't much better after bipartisan "Republicant's" fights, federal supplement refusals and compromises—we're back to square one with medical rip-offs—that look out for their rich investor(s) only. In their minds oddly, the wealthy make the world go around—what would we do without them, hail to the rich! ...because it's hell living with them.

So, how does momma get some beauty coverage with no insurance treasure booty? She retreats and she represses is what she does or find some quack knock-off not good enough makeshift physician or Walmart or Target's Beauty Shelves.

When people are depraved, they emotionally take on unrealistic standards to chase after alternative options because of lacking cash flow, e.g., weight loss in a bottle rip-offs, exotic melt-your-fat-instantly extractions, and plastic sweat clothes. They are like groping vultures after women's lacking confidence. She gets excluded from the commercially inane, vain, and rich game of fame only to feel dejected and fashionably lame she can't name her own fame. She shops bargain basements, Walmart, Dollar Stores, Family Dollars or sadly Rescue Missions, thrift, and vintage shops to find some semblance of trend and fashion. She dresses creatively by sewing her own.

When Madison Avenue sets a standard breast size and once the die is casted, well, that is it. There is no rebuttal on to the mag racks of endorsement catering to the privileged with 15 thru 20-year-old model bodies. Madison Ave is instant gospel and today's lifestyle. As far as the eye can see in every magazine or social ad, grocery checkout, online, billboard and Podcast commercial one cannot keep up with the latest trend; what's out and who's in; even Oprah can't keep up with Victoria Secrets. At the checkout counters, you get the luxurious opportunity to see what you *should* be looking like; how much you *should* weigh and if you were white this is the man you *should* be dating; or who you *should* hate because they married some Brown rap star. There at the check-out while waiting to pay for your Gator

Ade you will see what you're missing out on—
not being the new "normal."

Can anyone compete here?

Not even Madison Ave can keep up with
itself. The mechanisms of competition won't
allow it. This is probably why so many
executives get replaced or fired so often in
this industry and why so many executes are
mean spirited--fearing the bottom feeders
looking to climb.

Madison Avenue has stooped to ingénue
ages: 14, 15 & 16-year-old models to whom they
also photoshop and airbrush to find the
"perfect" but impossible "woman" one could
ever begin to envy. Sometimes the runway
models are so Auschwitz-thin that viewers are
not lamenting if they're eating but worried a
strong wind might wisp them away.

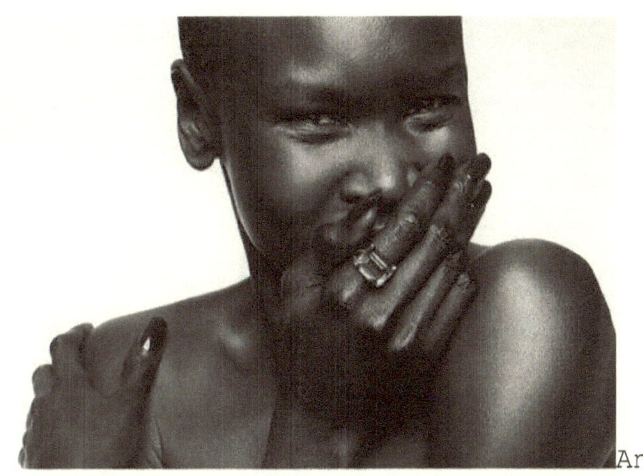And
it's not just the Brown women affected here
but all women are put under the pressure of
the neo-body Madison Avenue innovation "the
in-girl" standards.

I am not advocating the standardization
of obesity, poor eating habits and neglected
skin care or anything wildly negative. Neither
am I suggesting institutionalizing million-
dollar cosmetic health insurance policies that
cover Ms. Jekyll, Mrs. Hyde, and madam
"Frankenstina" facelifts as a necessary way of
keeping up with "Mad" standards.

Setting all that to the tune of
competition is another issue of inner self
love that will go absent. Can any women,
regardless of race, color or creed remain
psychologically and emotionally stable in such
a sexually orientated social chaos as this? Do
you think we'll drive our children into
neurosis with these expectations as they grow

into our modern commercially demanding adulthood madness? And will they up the ante once grown?

Let's re-examine this so-called cover girl marketing criteria. Models for the sake of effective sales have adversely derailed all women--to their own detriment given the latest controversy over emaciated looks and weight requirements. It's no wonder they're starving themselves thin to achieve ridiculous unrealistic sizes.

Dr. Oz use to present diversified holistic programs of general health practices daily that dealt with a wide range global healing method. Now daily, virtually every episode, is ALL about weight loss to keep his ratings up and meet the general program demands. They're all emotionally hurting themselves trying to attain the physically IMPOSSIBLE "normal" dream size. Women are not naturally a size 2.

I am not throwing Mad Ave under the bus… Wait, yes, I am throwing them under the bus, because they don't seem to have any idea of what's beautiful.

The social cultures that drive the competitive greedy cash cow makes them less than altruistic, supporting, and realistic about women's real needs but their fantasies—

for a buck at the expense of women's
psychological health.

Madison Avenue, the advertising "Mecca,"
and its fast-holding resurrection of "Aryan"
ideal influences, i.e., blond hair and blue
eyes, has a dead criterion for the third world
of ethnics. Blond hair and blue eyes are the
top of the line when defining beauty in
America—perhaps the world. It is the paragon
and hub of all beauty standards--so they'd
have you believe.

Where are they going with these feature
samplings and groupings?

We need to reject that broken CD from our
cache of racial importance. It does nothing
but mantra-repeat white noise in our minds on
things you will never attain easily. More
beauty expectations: slimmer, slimmer! Whiter!
Blonder! Thinner and thinner! Is a curse!

#

LOOK AGAIN CLEOPATRA

You are more beautiful than you think or know.
You will never ascertain, capture, or find
your idea of beauty if it's about something
else other than you. Why? Because you are
already beautiful. Just look again.

You're hoping for something you already
have. It is in your belief and acceptance of
yourself that you will find it. Look in the
mirror and say, "I love you. I accept you. You
are good enough for me and everyone else." Say
it relaxed and confident ten times a day like
you mean it. No, I mean it: say it ten times a
day. Trust it and believe it because there is

a take-home grab-bag at the end of this long
overdue pity party where you need to discover
you. Your esteem needs to be exercised by
saying it humbly in every reflection you see
yourself in. I'm not talking about
narcissistic aggrandizing egoistic vanity but
self-acceptance. "I like what God has made in
me." To verbally speak this out loud is to let
the universe go to work on your new beliefs.
In time, your body will adhere to what you
want to believe and become just that--
beautiful. You will see results in a month's
time or less. Again, I mean it.

This is not like taking an aspirin for a
20-minute relief. Esteem building takes some
input, from the heart, applied patience, soul,
and some time for the mind to all fall in love
with each other. Every physical cell needs the
time to set a new course to carry out its
given belief mission. And, when it happens,
love will blossom inward and outwardly.

Outer beauty without inward kindness,
excellent disposition and a peaceful soul is
like having a good government but hates its
people.

Love thyself:

*How can hair-naps and "the kitchen" be
made beautiful?*

How pretty is the blue infused in the white of your eyes?

How beautiful are white teeth against your dark and lovely skin?

How strong is your skin melon that keeps your skin from sagging?

Is there anything cuter than plaited hair dressed in barrettes?

#

BITCH IS AN UNNECESSARY EVOLVING CREATION

We cannot expect Brown women to passively deal with all this; in this current American climate without evolving into some stressed out and angry, back-talking, short patience, snarling, hand-on-hips neck rollin', nagging fuss-mouth social Medusa bitch.

How can they sustain these glass-ceiling blockages with a daily passive smile?

She can only keep Jesus staid on her mind for so long until somebody pushes her last nerve too far—and bam! One cuss-by coming up.

Again, granted most women cannot meet Madison Avenue ideals and society expectations. But, then again, if we insist on our answers lying in them (white racist) then it's not so much the shame on Mad Ave but blame on us for not taking the position of self-acceptance and reverse these self-incriminations--"So what the fuss?"[7]

Our forefathers who put this country together from scratch strongly advocated a society to which doors would be opened to all mankind (not women?) regardless of religion, race, or creed.

---

[7] Stevie Wonder, 2008

Lady liberty was intended to represent all to be welcomed and included among that same ideal democratic template, Madison Avenue was expected to do the same; include us. The first thing to be excluded from these liberties and privileges were also: Aborigine, Native Indians, East Indians, and native African beauty from advertising their beauty wares?

To be totally honest and fair, our "founding fathers" discriminated against white women initially and Brown women in turn had to pay their human dues and gained less liberation…

If you're truly loved and you know it—clap your hands. Even if you don't know when you're loved somehow you have nothing to lose; not knowing means someone has always loved accepted and respected you despite yourself. Love may appear absent among guarded hearts whose known love-disappointment but that never has to be registered or recognized as a lost because love, however dormant appearing, is always there.

There is an inner security and feeling of joy when you are loved. Perhaps we take it for granted but equally it is a much more noticeable feeling when the reverse feeling of love (hate) is a result of love being lost or eradicated from your heart; heartbreak, loneliness, or "motherless-ness." It's a hurt that's worst then any pain; not like a toothache or stubbed toe or a jarred funny bone but an unmovable pang in your soul that hurts deeply.

We all know that pain. When we lose love or a loved one is one longer there, we DEEPLY feel its absence. Well. this empty feeling is where many Brown people have known nationally, financially, and social love and political acceptance.

Why should the evolving bitch be nice, act right, be talkative, share, be considerate of others, learn to communicate cordially—what the heck for? Why would she blend in and create small talk, feel included and participate with the "mainstream," "odd-stream" or the bourgeois-dingalings; clearly, she's less than a minority being further "minored" politically.

When a socially, politically, or financially unloved lost soul sees the selected *fraternal* minded world (White privileged) it lives in, clearly and systematically it's an exercise to exclude her. This is where there is nothing to lose by having no cordial sensibilities or tact. So, they "bitch up."

Let's face it, "mainstream" means <u>members</u> <u>only</u>. Minorities see the game and sadly they admire the game—wishfully wanting to be included in the fun mostly stumped by the lack of money: can't attend the IVY league schools—no money, can't move up the corporate ladders—no clout, can't trade places with the gainful good o' boy investors—no legacy, can't get people to just spend money on their "stuff."—no economic support.

They can't sell drugs, can't pimp hoes and can't make too much cash at the altar without the IRS having questions. What other game is there for them to grope for? The Jesus games? We push that envelope to the max; at least, my Father in heaven loves me. But then there is the other Christians groping for the same thing, but only love each other provided they share the same pastor and show up at the same church of their membership and choosing. Otherwise, you might get a "God is good…" or a track of invitation.

Black people wish, hope and they pray all the time to be included but never truly feel like an invited participant of the "games." Sure, we make money playing professional ball but what do the owners earn?

Disrespect runs rapid, they disrespect our nation's ex-president. He can do nothing

correct without extreme criticism—even
bringing a 10-year war to an end and taking
out enemy #1 of the American people, Osama Ben
Laden. And even this isn't good enough for the
white racist majority.

Given these circumstances, it's not
apathy but the lack of fruitless energy to
even go on. Why? For what? To any other
humanity conscious society, it would sound
like a recipe for depressed suicide.

I suspect that's why so many inner-city
people are so susceptible to trend drugs; like
trailer park meth and pain-killer scams; they
too want relief from the "pangs" of going
"nowhere-dom" and feeling empty.

Who do you think you're foolin' Mr.
Joseph Goebbels (Hitler's Nazi assistant and
propaganda minister) who never fathomed the
joke would one day be on him and all his
deceptive and manipulative ways; he was
digging his own grave for himself and his
fuehrer (Hitler) completely unaware that **they
were themselves** digging two graves: one for
the Jews and one for their own historical
legacy of being the world's worst spiritless
idiots. They condemned their own memory to
dirt, worm, and rubble where all of Europe for
centuries to come would undyingly denounce

their family's name. [8]"What fools these mortals
be?"

Is this where we're headed with diabetic
insensitive foods, high blood pressures,
sugar, GMO plants, cancers, stress, minimum
wage and inner-city redlining (A designated
area). Again, would this be the new genocide?

#

---

[8] (A Midsummer Night's Dream, W. Shakespeare.)

YOU DON'T SEE ME

As a young man in college, in the mid 1970's, I was introduced to Al Jarreau. Although, I adored many of his recording I wondered curiously about the lyrics behind one of his songs. **"You Don't See Me,"** just what was he saying and was there a meaning to it all. I pulled the lyrics many years later:

You don't see me when I'm
trying to do right
Maybe you can see me now

When I was walking,
patting my feet on the pavement
Really, truly trying to find a gig
Did you stand up and speak
out in my favor?
Cold desperation,
she's a devil in bed
Scratching till my bones are bare
Pill and needles are all I've left to savor

We were walking and
I told you of how my shoes
Of how my shoes were wearing thin
You took your surplus and
traded for a favor
Now I'm demented and I'm
burned unto a cinder
Forty hours buys a grocery
bag for trash
I took my pistol and I made
myself a sinner

Will this universe be merciful at last?

You don't see me.
You don't see me
I get so tired of trying to
attract your attention
It has occurred to me that
you don't see me

You should go ahead.
I'm a-gonna-go-ahead
I know you're going to ahead
You're going to do what
you're going to do
I know, see, I see you, I watch you
You take the money and run

You take groceries and run, too
Don't leave nothing left for me
You're running and hiding
and ducking and hiding
And running and hiding and
I can't find you nowhere
I'll beat your mama,
I'll beat your daddy
I'll go to jail,
it don't make no mothafugging
Difference what happens to me
Going to be there in my
own time, in my own way
Cause you don't see me,
you don't see me
I'm, I'm in your mirror.

Since you don't see me for who I am or
you see me via lens to which you've been
influenced by stereotypical hyperbole, I never
get the chance to move pass your super-
privilege and power over me. For example, when

it comes to "business," I see that the
social/financial/political "fraternities"
(i.e., Good o' boys) they don't see me. For
many, there is a "cognitive dissonance"[9] (a
mental blockage that pretends one isn't there—
"you don't see me.") There are whites,
intrinsically, who don't care about us or want
to count us in. What they do see, our given
exceptional physical prowess. Especially when
we are 7 feet tall and can shoot a 40-foot
jumper with closed eyes or can rush 300 yards
a quarter; run 100 meters in 8 seconds; only
then are we somehow passionately VISIBLE. We
are a product of importance to their
gladiatorial thirst for competition; their
need for "bloodshed" and lust to win. It is
then, you see me pass your "cognitive
dissonance."

Sure, the Bouquet Race is fully aware
that once upon a time in "Camelot-America" we
could not attend or play sports in 1st division
schools or NFL, MLB, NBA and the shun the
thought we performed as quarterback—"team
leader."

Unlike today, a bygone era, Africans once
created their own Negro Leagues and 3rd
division schools where they could play. They

---

[9] See Post-Traumatic Slavery Dr. J. DeGruy-Leary

were never nationally recognized or affluent,
but they were ragingly popular ballplayers.

72

     Sure, after an arduous episode of civil
right wars to free Africans from oppression
and after a social war to free the "coloreds"
from constitutional distortion and ill civil
liberties--thanks to Martin Luther King, Jr.'s
sacrifice—this has allowed "Brothers" to play
ball in 1st division schools; with scholarships
and illegal non-endorsed NCAA "incentives"
(i.e., sport cars, straight cash, parental
jobs, etc.) to boot. Some of us have benefited
MLK's death and are living the dream. Many
"private boosters" (white cash cow
contributors who avoid NCAA recruiting
policies) are making it "do what it do" to
illegally get the "talent" to sign; where
Brown college kids are proud to advance their
opportunity and social horizons by signing—
it's all good in the 'hood.

     Ironically, after all those "wars," and
Martin's early demise, the majority players in

these 1st division schools are Black to whom
America openheartedly adores, loves, praises
and brags-and-"Shaqs" about. They've even
found fame, residual cash, endorsements, and
TV publicity; life is good; again, they're
living-the-dream--temporarily.

But wait a minute! What about the HBCU's
(Historically Black Colleges and Universities)
and their 3rd division status? If memory
serves, these schools came in existence
because 1st division schools, once upon a time,
would not allow Negros from the South or North
to attend their schools or play for them…once
upon a time in Camelot.

Have we've excluded or forgotten the 3rd
division school now?

When did we cease to love, praise, and
sell chicken dinners to raise money for their
benefit and reason to play ball too?

What about some social publicity for
these monumental Negro-American icons of
higher African liberation and learning
institutions?

Have we developed ama-dam-nesia
(Amnesia)?

Most 3rd division Black Colleges don't
significantly make the front page of their own
local newspapers let alone the national
mainstream…!

Is anybody Black or White paying attention?

Have Blacks developed a reverse "Cognitive Dissonance"?

Our baby boy or girl got a chance to step up so should I dismiss your ongoing blight?

Are the Black high schools and HBCU's a farm team for the big league (Top Ten)?

Our Brown athletes play the other side of the once restricted athletic fence; oh yes, Browns without a doubt abundantly approve of this with celebratory zeal! Much love is expressed for the Browns at the Florida Gator-Georgia Dog games. Even though, they (Whites) arrive in abundance with their Confederate flag's symbols and southern "obilia" displayed proudly. Has anybody asked the question with racism being as crazy a state of mind as any mental illness can be: "Do these psychopaths see black athletic induction as post-slave ownership? If no, why the Confederate flags at the games? The Confederate flag is a symbol of U.S. of A. rebellion to maintain a life of free labor off the backs of bought and pay for human-beings.

For Browns, they call college recruitment and drafts big progress. There's nothing like the anticipation of draft picks for Brown families. Its hope for the future; a chance to

get ahead! They play hard all 4 years or less
in the visible white schools and family
members sit by that telephone waiting for that
GM CALL. This is when they generally get a
white agent to walk them through it all, a
brand-new gabardine suit, and a jersey number
of their own.

They will recruit our Brown boys, and
this is GREAT, but on the same token they will
not fill our 3rd division stadiums and buy a
cold one or look at our pretty cheer leaders.
What is up with that kind of brazen hate?

Where are the vicarious sportsmen and
their painted nipples and crazed-out game
behavior for the Grambling or Bison brothers?
Where's that fanatic naked in winter fever and
subzero-cold weather with our local HBCU
colors and enthusiasm?

Oh yes! Tailgating park-outs. Why aren't
mainstream America parking their RV's a **week
in advance** at the HBCU's stadium classics like
their own 1st and 2nd division games? What kind
of "Elephant in the room" is this?

Is there an unspoken rule, "Ivy Leaguers
who did not matriculate at these colleges or
institutions, they are not allowed to have fun
among the Brown alumni school spirit?"

Yet, of late, most of "Ivy" players are
Brown—who knew!!

I have plenty of questions.

Why does it appear that whites need to see Browns as a distinct minority before they find comfort with their own presence? Why does TOO MANY Blacks make them nervous? What is this phenomenon? Have you gone to a game with a stadium of drunken young white men? It's dauntingly scary; DUI scary! They riot, vandalize, disrobe, beat each other to death, set property ablaze and get hit by moving vehicles walking along highways celebrating in drunken stupor. But whites are afraid of a HBCU "hoodie"?

All colleges and universities depend on money backed participation and support. Trust me, they do not discriminate your cash or your presence. It's simple economics. What's good for the White goose is equally the same for the Brown gander. Your ticket price goes to making a better way of life for all learning institutions, students, college employees, professors or cafeterias and bus persons. Green money doesn't discriminate, and it makes the world go economically around in the Brown neighborhoods also…

It's so important we all come out to the games—for communal morale's sake. Think what you want, but the U.S. is a democratic communal country. Sure, it is somewhat about the alumni spirit that they come, but they all participate and sometimes they get spiritually closer by celebrating team enthusiasm—camaraderie is exulted as they all cheer for their team and colors.

It's all about the rapport. They expand the human spirit as they cheer and rally with each other—socially bonding. Why not salute the source from whence these great athletes hail from—Black schools? Brown and Pink bodies should get to know NEGRO institutions. After all, this is where "mainstream" NFL is pulling a lot of their amazing talent. This is where the Michael Jordan to whom you love so much, and want to me like, hail from.

Let's stop this phony <u>Wizard of Oz</u>, behind the green curtain casting illusion propaganda crap, "Bring me my competitive enemies' ruby cleats" and I'll give you the secrets of the bio-computer (brain), Tin-man feelings and lionlike courage.

There are no big secrets great athletics don't already possess. It takes BRAINS to make his body do the amazing tricky things he/she performs--in their sleep. It takes FEELING passion to pursue something that doesn't want you and it takes a great deal of heart to have courage to walk up to "your unknown world" and fit in in-spite of demonic hate, hue-based prejudice, and handed-down ignorance. He doesn't need Oz to survive. …He is the wizard—he just doesn't know it.

When will all Brown people and other third world humans be just as important and worthy of Camelot-America to themselves as well as their need to feel included by whites?

Is there fear perhaps that 1st division schools will become our 3rd division schools…? I cannot speak for all HBCU's long term goals but rest your phobias my white audience that isn't even close on their bucket-list of Brown priorities. Again, Brown people just want to feel like the prodigal son or daughter, not racially judged, included, and not used.

All this has spawned a social phenomenon among Brown young athletes. They can't have outside the court or off the field privileges. So, they've taken to their White female colleagues and finding their liberation and acceptance there. Hence, the Brown woman is again Jack Johnson'd out of a life of abundance and plentitude but a candidate for another lesser monetary station.

Brother Prince when will you awake her from her coma sleep with your kiss? Or are you waiting for her to froggy kiss you back to manhood?

THE BODEGA BEAUTIES

Enough of that, let's return to Brown women and those compared with exceptional and extraordinary paragons of "Amazonic" strengths and looks.

There are white women "super models" that earn millions; the size 2 ideally where ONLY white women were privy to this status and economic base. Granted times are changing since I began researching for this book in 1992 where Brown-women DID NOT remotely earn those kinds of bucks for their physical attributes and wares; where management and talent agencies of Hollywood, Madison Avenue of Manhattan namely avoided Brown women like Catholic science, molestation, and liberal politics.

They avoided their existence through images, mass media and propaganda. Before I go on, what might that be--propaganda? It is a design but self-induced art of persuasions which means getting one to do something without directly alluring them to do something or not. Madison Avenue was driven, or better pressured, not to pay Brown women the same dollars per hour, by comparison in

commercials, cable, T.V., or print ads to
attract the very same audience—classic glass
ceiling exposure and pay. And clearly the
persuasion was Browns did not compare with the
apex charms of white American beauty. Even if
they had to draw the images of perfect bodies—
which they did:

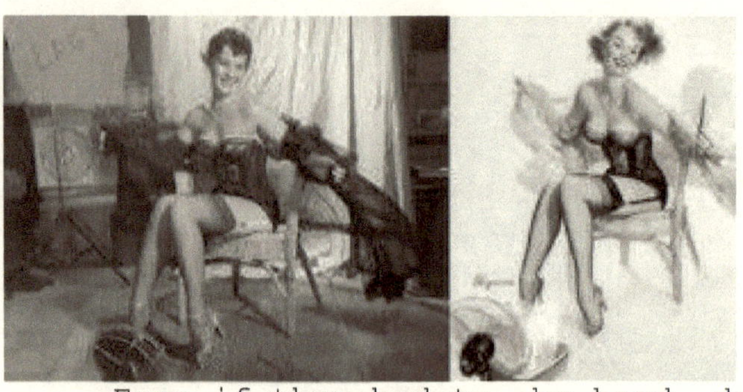

Even if they had to, by hand, draw the image they longed for they did so to persuade the world their white beauty could and would never compare to the American woman. These sizes are unreal. I can prove it by Dr. Oz's program obsession with weight lost and body shaping of late. As a result of these above ideal cultures women are led to believe something is wrong with their bodies because they don't naturally look like the photo-shop and drawings their grandmothers in their youth once had.

Today this is called photo-shopping or cropping. It is an image app that allows a photographer to reshape, fix blemishes and perfecto a person.

Once upon a time, in the 1970's, a Brown super-model was an anomaly—some rare find. She was either less attractive with other dynamic physical stuff or she was pretty but with weight issues.

There was always the question, "Did Brown women have the same appeal to motivate and drive sales among the populace, the mad sale hoppers, the wealthy daylight euro-shoppers and have the physical "props" to sexually attract male audiences and be the envy of a female admirer?" Could she make white women jealous and white men horny? Prior to the millennium change of 2003, Brown Woman were not readily seen in advertisements selling soda, beer, sports cars and certainly not the late 1960's Noxzema Medicated comfort shave ads— "Take it off. Take it all off." That was limited to Sweden women only.

(http://youtu.be/EkpGM MvZ2Y), or the Van

Heusen shirt ads,

(http://youtu.be/XXP74qdw6-o), and of course

Tyra Banks the first Black woman to cover GQ

and Sports illustrate; and her competitor
Naomi Campbell.

    Are Brown models demographically used to
attract Black men in TV target ads? I say,
yes.

    They can be seen in bodegas (Spanish
markets), mini-marts, confectionaries or where
beer is sold in urban neighborhood convenient
stores only. Budweiser, for example, have
printed honorable posters of great African
Kings (Of Africa) such as Hannibal:

the
Carthaginian North African general that
defeated Rome for 14 years. Or, Shaka Zulu,
the South African Zulu king who out foxed and
defeated the colonizing British Empire and
enslave their British officers for decades
before his decided release. There in bold
print, on local (Hood) store window fronts and
stock walls of these stores' true Black

history ads with sole intent of selling a
demographic Brown consumer:

"My beer is Rheingold..."

says *Dorothy Dandridge*

Extra refreshing because it's Extra Dry!

You enjoy all the extras in every glass of Rheingold Extra Dry. The bright, clear look of it. The fine bouquet of it. The clean, crisp taste of it—extra refreshing, extra satisfying. Today—treat yourself to Rheingold. You'll know why so many millions like the *dry* beer best. It's New York's largest-selling beer.

TUNE IN JACKIE ROBINSON ON RADIO—PRESENTED BY RHEINGOLD 6 TIMES A WEEK! See your newspaper for time and station.

However, white businesses have not, in my purview, placed similar images in front of their own stores. Yet, without prejudice,

Browns continue to trade there, hoping mostly
for social inclusion.

Without a doubt, white women, or any
attractive woman, will do for the local Brown
stores but for some deeply "racist" reason
it's not well enough for the white consumers
and their store fronts. She (Brown models)
doesn't exist.

Does white-America fear they must resist
this "propaganda" that these images will lead
them down a path to hell? Do they really think
Brown people, all people, aren't aware of
these misleading images of deception that all
men, here in America, are NOT equal in the
land of the free?

Are white models used to attract black
males for business?

Are Brown models used to attract white

male for business?

Thanks to Beyonce

and "Scandal"
(TV series), maybe there is a chance.

Do you think Brown women might feel undermined given our current marketing mainstream?

Let's reflect again on self-love and the theory that no one can be responsible for another's self-appreciation: the power of influence and/or the powers of social exclusion can never lift the already existing feeling of worthlessness. With these blatant absent images of "browness," I would think many feel isolated.

Hans Christian Anderson wrote the children's tale, "The Ugly Duckling" because it was initially a black duckling that later blossomed white and beautiful founding its way out of its darkness.

This is more than a solid reason for social and clinical depression—to which any Brown people might fall into and suffer.

However, White depression comes from many things, bio-chemicals and other circumstances and substances but certainly not from the feelings of exclusion where they might imagine, "I'm not good enough." Whites, feelings of being privileged, are generally innate.

The world envies white-American's feelings of freedom that the sky is indeed the limit. They are free to go as far as education, opportunity and hard work will take them.

What better feeling in life to know your business is always backed by someone, my investments and your welfare is always looked out for; my political opinions are equally encouraged.

However, at this very moment, as I write these very words, although I too am an

American, I fear that Browns won't read this because whites won't endorse it—so I write not for profit or fame but regurgitation and outlet.

Equally, whites won't read it because it appears Black and has nothing to do with "them" or anything they can respect.

Mexicans and Asians do not have to encourage whites to support their business.

What part of the American dream do I have?

To be fair, racism has minimized Brown people but from where I stand since 2013 the Brown woman hasn't had overwhelming representation for the eyes of all men. Whenever "big businesses" refer to major ad campaigns, serious business for major money markets—for real deal stuff—where they mean to appeal to the elite's check books, money is everything and the "right images" must be applied. Wherever money is a risk, image becomes a matter of life and death, and blond is queen: news and weather reporters, diaper commercials, health ads, political campaigners, or their wives; even public service announcements, white women dye their hair blond for "successful" business matters. Brown women represented by these major endeavors or major markets have been risky in the eyes of the advertiser. Our own former Governor of Florida (Rick Scott) during his first term campaign minimized public photo opts with his then Lieutenant Governor, Jennifer Carroll, a Black woman, and conservative republican, until his success as governor was solidified in 2011.

Who was he fooling?

He was appealing to his Floridian racist base. They were trying to avoid the obvious and overwhelming prejudice in his own Red State by taking no chances of fraternizing with a Republican Brown woman. After all, how can there be a debate on eradicating a Confederate Flag that flies over our state buildings in the south with a Brown woman as your Lieutenant Governor?

Governor Scott has since dumped Ms. Carroll, allegedly, because of a money scandal that she probably took the fall for allegedly—don't quote me here.

And later, Gov. Rick Scott used Carlos-Lopez Cantera for all the Hispanic, Mexican and Cuban contingencies that they also ticked off during his first 2011 election by throwing them under the bus trying to look tough among other conservative "cray-cray"[10] bigots and gain their confidence and votes.

Spokeswomen, models, and actresses that hold the reigns for selling power and influence, do not take the risk on Browns. In some defense, it's getting better but mo' better can be done. Beautiful Brown women are Americans too and they have earned the right to swan from their too long "...duckling status.

#

---

[10] Larry Wilmore of the Comedy Channel code word for "Political craziness"

Beauty is registered from the mind or imagination of the beholder. Has Madison Avenue beheld the ethnic Brown woman as the delicate, angelic-like damsel in distress, so innocent and so pure?

Again, in fairness, they are getting better but at a snail's pace for my money.

How many diverse television shows and
movies are there about ethnic Brown woman
depicted as focal stars? What about Native
African women as Hollywood stars? Surely, we
can agree, they are the first American woman.

Now, on the
other hand, I can list hundreds of foreign,
defected, migrated Australian and European
found Hollywood stars—endless samplings and
varieties. However, I don't have a similar
American
list for East Indians,

Hawaiians

Aborigines (Below),

Egyptian (Above)
  Spanish,

Asians (Yes, many),

Mexicans

and South American starlets.

If your answer is, "I think so" or "I count many," reconsidering your count since the dawn of TV (1950's) and screen (Turn of the 20th century) that's pretty sad. Count again: what's your count now?

I don't mean not to be unreasonable; it has gotten better since the 1950's, the 60's event and the 80's but compared to what is standard and why the slow growth depresses the mind of the 3rd world and non-whites, it's very sad.

Thank god for BET, Centric and OWN cable and Univision Telemundo-Spanish network channels, and Black Lives Matter movements. Minute as it may seem, there are some outlets

to allow some feelings of *inclusion* among
ethnic women. Granted, the numbers have been
increasing and the world is happier for it—we
all want to work, eat, and feel admired.
However, something is still yet remiss… With
all the talent, beauty and intelligence of
Brown women everywhere there should be more
celebration of her external and inner
(creative) beauty. After all, compared to the
above listed beauties, African's have been
around historically longer than all our
evolving species--for what it's worth. There
must be some earthly seniority considered.

Isn't seniority a way we're supposed to
represent "stardom" or the "workplace"? The
Kennedy Center salutes honorees for their long
stay, outstanding talents and humanitarian
contributions. The way we seem to view the
seniority of White Hollywood stars—the
pioneers, the honored and the privileged; the
Oscar seem to uphold my point. They reward
those who worked hard, have given their best
and have come this far with deserving kudos.
Since they've paid their dues, we salute them,
recognize them. And what does that do for
their esteem? It does wonders.

But, why does that not apply to Brown
people considering their hard work, long
standing and not to mention historical origin?

JUST WHO IS THE BROWN MOTHER'S "BODYGUARD"?

According to popular inside Hollywood reports, Kevin Costner was considered "brave" to inter-race relate with a love interest in the acclaimed movie, "Bodyguard." With then, the beautiful and very capable Whitney Houston both Kevin and her starred. Just what potential political pitfall could Mr. Costner have been jeopardized with by such a "brave" endeavor? The man was then a mega-star and projected zillionaire. What could he potentially loose by this racial mesh?

Where are we going with this racial exclusion?

Clearly time has proven Brown people cannot be stopped--and what's to stop by the way? --and why would you? Racism clearly is a puppy catching its tail.

What risk Kevin? Would he had Lost some good-o-boy seal of approval or carrying card? Who and where is this good-o-boys (or girl) caucus? Who's monitoring miscegenation regulations? He was "Brave…?"[11] Did this

---

[11] William Earl, Blogger 2012 Houston's funeral

bravery dare to be thrown out of the "White gentlemen's club?" Perhaps eradicated from the White girl's hunk list? Was/is the film industry insinuating a *fictitious* love affair between **actors** would be politically risky because of their color difference? Could he have lost some endorsements? Would something like this depress white America, white women potentially spoiling Mr. Costner's career to have shared a romantic experience with an African woman from Newark, NJ? I am sorry about all the questions, but inquiring mind must know.

I know Brown women that still watch this film in secret (my own wife included) to this day—it's the perfect tissue box chic movie flick made in 1992--NOT 1865, where we passed a law for freedom, but the kidney stones of racial restrictions continue to pang our social groin.

Is this really what we are wasting our Zoloft on?

Tom Cruise didn't blink when the opportunity came up to kiss Thandie Newton

in "Mission Impossible II"—but, then again, he's a Scientologist and along with racism they (the racist) probably hated him doing that too.

Does Brown woman need a Thandie English accent for her charms to be appreciated?

Perhaps I am thinking too negatively but let me flip the script a bit for the sake of fairness. The world is in fact 9/10 inhabited by people of color. What if that 9/10 played the same nefarious and underling games of superiority on the 1/10 white population to further remind them of their minority and inferiority less than valued status? Are we creating our own societal depression here with these inane obsessions…?

Now, don't run out to purchase an AK47 to hurt anyone. This is not some Nazi prelude to 1/10 genocide—that's crazy talk and crazier thinking. People of color just want American INCLUSION without the games based on prejudice, segregation, and discrimination. And don't tell me, "you hadda' Black president; what more do ya' want?" --not when political and journalist racist attacked him both terms!

No, we had a good president and why not have more.

What about the Brown woman's depression?

To get through the day, she must be suffering some sort of cognitive dissonance having to pretend racism doesn't exist. Either that or she must live with such terroristic realities daily.

No embryo chooses their colour.

Just what should a mother's dreams be for her baby given this culture? What does she tell her baby? "Well kids, you gotta bad poker hand, so bluff"?

Like Sisaundra Lewis from TV talent search, The Voice (2014 contestant) who was clearly an empress of song, a major voice and muse-voice but was not good enough for America—after she choose the country-western singer trainer/judge to be her coach. She was MORTIFIED by America who clearly voted their prejudice. My white friends were mad as hell at those obvious racist votes. Even the contestant who won, their 2nd choice, was disappointed at white American demographic votes as well--she was visibly SHOCKED. She didn't want to win that way—on the strength of a lie.

To be racist is one thing, but to be race-competitive in America in these so-called United States is a social disaster—no wonder Edward Snowden and Donald Trump feel exonerated and uncommitted to their country. Our secrets aren't safe with them because

there no real allegiance for them to attach
to.

What union is this when we allow racist to befriend us?

Turn them off, turn away, run away, or
walk away from them.

How do you think that affects a society
of Brown people discovering they're yet
stained and tainted with no Kennedy, Malcolm,
Nina Simone, or Martin to stand up for them,
protect them, sing protest for them, speak for
them, or guide them? Let's face it; our former
president Obama was terrified of the topic of
race. He made a good point, "Race: there is
nothing to talk about but to do something
about."[12] That is his biggest elephant in the
social and political rooms of America.

Kanye and Kim aren't catching social hell
because she screwed a man now on YouTube's
video (How many women get dupe into those
scandals?). And so, what if she is an
attention camera junkie—who isn't in show-
business? They bully her because of Kanye—the
black guy; of course, attacking Taylor Swift
on national TV didn't help; although, he made
a good point: Beyonce is dope. They feel he's

---

[12] 2015 Charleston, SC eulogy for Senator Pinckney

an arrogant outspoken black man who spoke the truth to President Bush during the Katrina Hurricane Relief Telecast: "He doesn't care about Black people." This is what he said…although, he was right, Bush did not. What, no freedom of speech for Kanye?

Kim is a drop-dead glorious Armenian woman who loves Brown men; there lies the real American hate base. White America largely considers her not to be a worthy entertainment leader and certainly not their "precious."

What's next; take pot shots at their beautiful mixed babies? That should be the drawn line in the sand where we Americans say, "Stop it now!!"

America failing to include Brown women is when the gangster hip-hoppers and booty pimps take over and turn our damsels-in-esteem-distress into video pole dancers where their value is to shake that-a… and not so much their talents. Even Ike Turner did a more dignified job there, a brutal pimp nonetheless, but he drove her off well and revered.

Social exclusion is spiritual genocide on all fronts. These short-stops and thwarts the inner beauty of ANY woman of any color. There is insurmountable evidence in Bosnia, Croatia,

Romania, the bowels of North Korea and Russian
and Turkey where esteem depletion is
catastrophic. People are exploited and pimped
daily, i.e., human trafficking, even the
children are turned out to trick (solicit) for
parents.

Again, considering all the amazing women
Mr. Costner is privy to kiss and fall in love
with, if he so desires, Whitney was not a
bust. Costner, a man of privilege, boosting
the confidence of a major Brown woman, one of
the greatest songstresses ever and EVER;
infinitely included forever in the diva's hall
of fame. I say kudos to Kevin and Whitney and
"hear-hear" to the spiritual health of ethnic
women and white. This is a blade that cuts
both ways. What heals one heals the other

Clearly, we are all Americans.

White people aren't responsible for the health
of Brown womankind. And Browns are no less
responsible for white woman skin not being

able to work the cotton fields. But however,
we should be responsible to each other. Can we
also be responsible for damaging social
isolation and physical discrimination felt by
everybody?

Are we not our sister's keeper too?

After all the police bludgeon abuse,
baton caused concussions and foot-stomped
brain damage, Rodney King's cheese did slip-
off-of-his-cracker, but his simple words of
forgiveness were noble, "Can't we all just get
along?" This is not rocket science; the more
we fight for separation and social isolation
the more it seems to forge our Brown boys and
white girls to grope after each other. Our
White women and Brown men apparently attracted
to each other, and they like it. There are a
lot of beautiful be-loved Brown babies around
to qualify that point. The universe, God, or
the great-Amoeba obvious agrees with it.

The KKK advocates adamantly races can be
friends but no mixing of the races: is the
French and German a mix? Swedes and the
English? Austrians and Northern Italians?
Prince Harry and Meghan Markle?

What is incest among them if that's not mixing?

Perhaps they should have considered this non-mixing policy 200 years ago while violating African women at their leisure, creating millions of light-skin Negroes in America, the Caribbean, Central and South America; we have too many mulattoes to refute that fact. There is so much ancient mixing among Cubans, and South American "Spanish," some don't know that they're Black. It is, KKK, what it was—this is YOUR created Frankenstein that you ironically despise.

Look, we all pay the Hollywood entertainment industry for their good works. Is Kevin racially beholding to one demographic audience more than another—as we live and breathe in the same country? Did he or the producers worry, "What will my White friends think if we co-star a Black icon?"

Did other singers turned actress have these issues like: a Jewish Barbara Streisand, an Italian Madonna, a Southern-Bell Britney Spears, Cali-girls Jessica Simpson and Cher or Mid-Western Dolly Parton? Should they have not kissed leading man? Raquel Welch and Jim Brown did. Are the KKK invested, supporting, and sponsoring the entertainment industry?

Are we perforated into convenient divides of Whites, Browns, Native-Americans, Asians, and Spanish worlds within the same country when it comes to Hollywood and kissing?

I can only imagine how exhausted racist people must be from all this racial tail-chasing. Clearly, it is a lesson in futility. Poor babies, they run to the rural suburbs and then back to re-gentrify our inner cities: back to the woods and the GMO farms, and back to the organic farms and back to renovating abandoned warehouses and shore docks; all the while redlining (neighborhood designating) ethnic groups as the white-privilege property-hop forcing "minorities" to migrate where depleted, polluted and exploited now dwell.

Were Hollywood executives so shallow and afraid that their cash cow Golden Boy (Costner) will be thrown out of some "privileged" fraternities; blackballed, branded, de-boned, stoned and left for politically dead if he kisses a Brown woman publicly?

For shame, they'd do such a horrendous thing without a proper farm-shed to do it in.

Did Michael Jackson fear this same political paradox; with Lisa Marie Presley, or "his children" by a European foreign surrogate mother and all his surgeries and hair straightening perms?

I loved Michael like I love yesterday's marinated and rubbed ribs, and so did the world adore him, but really? Did Michael love Michael (himself) as well or as much as we did? Perhaps he wanted to be bleached from his darkness but less the cause by vitiligo ironically.

As long as I can remember, as a child, The Colored, the Negros, longed and fantasized to be white-like that they might, by second choice, be light-skinned to be considered attractive and beautiful: to be white was to be loved and nationally included.

I wrote these following notes in 1992 while complying data for this book: "Considering the diverse ethnic growth of the movie industry, politics, and the growth of our economy among Browns, will Mr. Costner want to be found guilty of such a "McCarthy" like past in his crowning years of the 21st century?" Even Ralph Waite

who played a wanton fang dripping slave cargo sailor, and rapist, redeemed himself with the role in "The Bodyguard" film as Kevin's stage-dad is now a changed man.

It was then the 21st century with a 2nd term Brown president that we might be civilly evolving—who would have ever thought. And, the very woman Kevin politically struggled to kiss, there he stood at her home-going funeral testifying, with a heavy heart, his adoration for her greatness, kindness and his own personal lost by her death. I speculate to believe that Whitney was probably a catalyst for his racial maturity as well as professional friendship.

I ask how a Brown woman functions emotionally with these Oliver Twist like slaps in the face. Their behavior has become a conditioned response of anger by no fault of their own; social numbness is their only mechanism for coping with racial stress and dissonance?

Or does she have the emotional energy to respond to this blight, or can she emotionally afford to, without being labeled? Where does she get her love, acceptance, needs and wants fulfilled?

Is anybody listening to her?

Women in general are starting to get their due respect in entertainment; however slowly. Although Brown people are struggling minorities, they are working well, or it is improving--getting better, as it were.

I don't for a second think they are not aware of this "minoritizing," having the lesser vote and last word that counts. They know they're not readily "membered" into the Hollywood "Fat Cat's" craw; let's call it what it is: it's a putdown for Brown women.

Who is the Wizard of Hollywood who decides selectively who is going to work so they can eat in their cornucopia film Industry? -Harvey Weinstein? How in Hades are they paying some actors individually $20 million a film when Browns and many White actors too are starving. What kind of fools do they think we are that we don't see their end games? We are aware of their hunger-games.

They know, or should quickly learn, all this arrogance will come-a-tumblin' down someday if this continues? There is plenty of work for "minorities" in film, especially with the number of films being made yearly. HBO, Hulu, Netflix and video streaming will never run out of material. Hollywood is simply a business that demographically weights and measures the yield of money preference. They monitor the desires and trends of the majority big-spenders and all their discriminations as well, Or they flatly tell us what we like.

        Check the magazines at the checkout
grocer counters it doesn't matter whether they
(white stars and celebrities) are doing bad,
behaving ugly, obese, scandalized, or even
molesting the young. They make the front-page
cover above Brown people for us to read as we
wait; with the exception of OJ and now Cosby.

This is not healthy for anyone as they ignore
Browns and lie to themselves that Browns don't
exist.

What about Brown men?

**What's her response to some of their ill-
nurtured social behaviour?**

BUT YOU WANTED THE TRASH?!

If the truth be told, all women deal with so-called ideal physical expectations for commercial mainstream in both business and the public. But I submit that Brown women deal more so. They have for hundreds of years had to cope being the last to be considered for stardom; reduced to be the help. I can only imagine that's why "The Help," the movie, was written to show the 20th century 2nd class female laborer's worth putting the value of self-esteem in others before herself; coping with what was expected of them with limitations they were given and socially reminded of, both in the north & South, e.g., my own family. This became their station in "this" life from the 1940's through the 1970's.

If it isn't their skin being too dark, it's their hair not being straight, blond, or they are "a bit too overweight," and hair too nappy; something was never quite good enough. And, I am not blaming whites here.

Her domestic suppression was and is no stranger to Black men who *sometimes* lend a hand to lessen her feelings of disparity.

Let's face it, there aren't a lot of male
lobbyists out there protesting, rallying,
shaking pompoms, sounding air-horns and
rocking the boat on her behalf to triumph pass
color lines to gain her rightful and deserved
"queendomship." However, she's ALWAYS "rocked-
da-boat" for him though—unfailingly and
thanklessly.

Brown women cope with all these glass
ceiling metaphors and social obstacles; second
to the existing issues of white women. And to
cope, Brown women have become famous for
pulling their shoulders back, lifting their
heads high and being confident with whatever
challenges may come--in spite of racial
American craziness.

They've developed emotional strengths most of us couldn't begin to brag about: saying no to a child who needs shoes, visiting a life sentenced husband or family member, welcoming a son's blond lover whose parents might dare to accept him, giving a "crack-head" brother a place to stay or laying with a man she doesn't "love" but he's able to pay a light-bill; all for the security of her children…

All women want special praise, recognition and s "sweet" companion who says, and does, nice things. It's human to want to be married and bonded in matrimony. A wedding first and children later is an ideal highlight of her life, a perfect life for many. She likes something she can care for; care about, and wholeheartedly love. She wants a mate who *equally* cares for her in exchange. Sometimes affection will do, and she'll do the work.

I am not a woman, but I think betrayal hurts them deeply once they've given you, their heart. It's especially painful when she loses her mate's respect to some substance-less "drag-nasty" (deadbeat types) or sub-fantasies (cheat experiences) that has no real home-training, nothing going on but more useless BS and unproductive "trash"—the usual baseless suspects. This hurts anyone: men, women and especially children when there is NO human credence in our day-to-day drive to survive. All this can be apathetically damaging.

Even if the deadbeat is a woman, this equally can be debilitating, and it reduces her ego and children around her. To be picked over for some indecent, low, and trash-mouth type with no class can only lead to provocative violence and extreme stress. What she needs, and what we should want for her, are productive social experiences less absent of joy, fun and good times.

Any social base with any above negativity erodes us from the core having to be something we aren't to be included. Having to strive for unreal images to be "like," the Madison Avenue lifeless "super models" types where women compete with choices made over the fantasy of unrealistic dress sizes by way of malnutrition that damage their health is ridiculous. No way. We should stay away from that. Perhaps the idea that Mad-Ave might think they aren't "appealing enough" might well be a blessing for them.

How can anybody compete with such a head trip?

Women starve themselves to appeal to some American-male sexual libido, appealing to some crazed ideal physical type. How does the Brown woman grow a flat ass or even develop a real derriere without toxic chemical assistance?

Oh, and there are the domestic (homely) expectations?

You know, the energy to maintain a household with children and all the thankless duties of keeping a family together; her trying to look perfectly fabulous or most times settling for a little exercise called washing and food shopping. It's a no-win situation unless she has undying dedicated support from her mate and all his loyalty.

She will never pull it off unless there is a support system that is encouraging and cheering her on about the ups and downs of life, stuff, and things; all the trial and errors of weight loss and self-reinvention are worth it when there is help from a mate. This is true love and love is "fuel" to humans.

It is very difficult and extremely stressful when that "fuel" is not committed solidly, or with longevity. She needs someone who sees her realities and accepts them for what they, and she, are in times of challenges. She doesn't see her own fruit unfolding, blossoming beautiful and availing at first. A lot of women don't have the ability to see their potential beauty. My own wife gets up from breakfast on Sunday morning and charges in to dress for church service. 40 minutes later, she will emerge with a look of complete despondency. She will ask the next question vulnerable and with total dependency, "How do I look?" It is at that precious moment she awaits her validation by my words: "Honey, you look wonderful" and if I light-up with a smile, her good mood is set for the day. From that moment on the world is alright with her and endowment is rooted in my ordainment,

love, and approval. We all need our loved
one's reassurance.

This must be reinforced with regularity
endorsing friends, family and especially mates
and partners as well.

When her mate says, "Honey you look
sexy." However sometimes after a long day of
work, her typical response can easily be, "My
Lord, where's your glasses."

Why, doesn't she always feel beautiful?
Well, there are many reasons for that.
However, many women, to look beautiful, they
must first FEEL beautiful in them self.
Remember the movie, "Carrie," by pretense the
"prince" who was coerced into convincing her
of her beauty only to be betrayed by the
"prince's" girlfriend with the bloody bucket
of ridicule. This is what our American society
and our Brown selves have done to the Africa
woman—we've "Carried-her." A bucket of blood
has been thrown on her hope for social
acceptance and peer fantasies--I don't know
where Serena Williams gets the strength but
now that she's had a beautiful mulatto baby.
It's a bit clear what she might have been
going through during her years of athletic
triumph that America might not do the same to
her endorsed child.

We have set the African up for the blindsiding bucket when we sing love songs to her but grope after white "ideal" sexual images—who by the way are struggling too. When Brown men sleep with her in the dark but trophies' the white chic in the light, this is a blood-bucket on the Brown woman. They are publicly good enough to be "used" but not good enough to be flaunted.

Let's face it. We Brown men have created too many "Carries" and they are pissed off with their hands-on hips and their angry necks are rotating.

And we wonder why her "bitch" thrashes out to attack, on cue. She is angry—fair enough. Nobody likes a "bitcher" not even "bitches."

This is where the communal smiles have gone from our culture, the cute chuckles of laughter in the wind, flirtatious eye lash waves filled with happiness as friends drive by with decorated, unsolicited hellos and genuine selfless greetings, public nods, social hugs, and humble meekness to kudos mentioned. What you got instead are the gorgeous "Housewives of Atlanta" and all that socially pent-up learned venom to boot. They are angry!

    This is not just a Brown thing.
Similarly, White women struggle with this more
than anyone—HIGH expectation of perfectionism—
to be blond, be a size 2, be a DD cup and
perky, and be without hair from the blond dye
or coloring; so many destroy their hair
follicles and risk skin cancer with excessive
sun exposure just to temporarily be brown for
a short summertime. They too perpetuate images
they fail to keep up with; one trend after
another reaching for unattainable physical
goals that don't exist; never realizing that
beauty is a result of loving yourself and
accepting who you are with a little help from
her friends— "You look wonderful."

    On the other hand, White women do not set
any bars of perfectionism. The woman's image
can only be effective if the White or Brown
man is moved and aroused—that's the only real-
world criteria. If that muse isn't there, game
over. It is for naught—it's ALL about sex.
That's what sells. But RACISM trumps sex. This
is where the bottom-line is NO LONGER the
bottom-line and the buck is not stopped but
rejected.

    The Brown man's sexual attention to the
Brown woman's attributes and physical detail
with more emotional commitment removes all
doubts and anxieties with clear distinction.

It will fix any racial disparities the Brown
women might have to compete with. But the most
important question is: where's the love for
whom and what you are?

More love directed to her and less lust
on his part, groping after every white woman,
not seeing the bigger picture where Brown
women are, and she is excluded for designed
racial purposes, can be esteem healing. Yes
brother, a lot is in your hands. Don't expect
miracles, but it's a start. If the Brown man
can praise and prize her, without any closet
surprise, she'll find exclusion from any
mainstream tolerable. "She must be
appreciated, never tolerated."[13] That's healing
love.

It's not so much the mom who catches her
son, or husband, pleasuring, arousing himself
or masturbating. But it's white sexual
contraband (porno). It's the "blond" choices
he chooses whose culture do not regard him in
the same manner. Psychologically, this hurt
and damages her esteem.

No one improves under the pressure of
physical perfection—there is no such thing;
just great health is what's attractive; a
healthy person is a good-looking person.

---

[13] Cousin Bessie Mae Brown, Valdosta, Ga., July 2015

Unlike any female, Brown women have withstood all kinds of romantic rejections. Women love to "have sex" but most, I've researched, would rather to be made love to-- there is a difference. And it begins with "can't take my eyes off you heat." That act is better consented through genuine, mutual attraction and social rapport that one loves another for oneself.

White women, all women, catch this same kind of hell because of their intrinsic need to please others and the general society they live among. Women like to behave and be regarded as model citizens of decency and order—which is often based in religion, making it a guilt driven mandate among most.

Many men put a great deal of pressure on women by over engaging on their imitated fantasies played out on massive mag-covers. Brown women see these choice magazine images and online naughty(s) as competition. They observe our male-eyes as we lust over the "heated" pages and centerfolds. Or, when we scan the joint for nice big butts--they're on to our dark shades at the beach or the mall. Sure, it's natural for males to girl-watch but sometimes at the cost of emotional orphanage and rejected shame. What must she do: wear Asian wigs, sewed in weaves, apply tattoos on her dark canvas-skin, gold grill their teeth, eye lashes that lap a breeze in the wind, thong short booty-shorts, multi-inch painted nails, 2 sizes too tight yoga-spanx; put-outs without any promissory husbandry? How long do we make her wait to fulfill her rightful need to be loved— "fueled" as it were?

Men are a little too taken by these insistent male-American fantasies to notice what she needs. I assure you it is not unrealistic bewitchments of perfumes and unattainable body-perfect physical expectations.

Playboy bunnies are vehemently sought after, high, and low, far, and wide, to find the "perfect ten." The mag photos are the final matrix after hours of auditions. Advertisements work HARD on what men are supposed to believe and are led to believe what is typical or the normal. No, Victoria Secret is an illusion, dude. Their "secret" is our gullibility to be easily deceived. Finding Waldo's daughter in lingerie is a Big Foot, Abominable Snowman, and Unicorn hunt. She doesn't readily exist. She is mostly airbrushed.

If men find that's hard to believe that there are many perfect girls out there, look again at yourself and compare what you see to a NFL athlete, WWF wrestlers and the amount of effort and driven years it takes to develop such a 6-pack physique. Are you a perfect ten, sir? Not even close: your hair needs a cut, eyebrows and mustache need trimming, your shirt is probably un-ironed drip-dried and faded or you wear nothing but t-shirts, ran-over flip-flops, lotion needed legs and feet, nails are grease-dirty, ain't done a seat-up in years, knee socks with sandals and she still copes with us and all our male short-comings… The difference with her is she'll settle for our 3 pack abs for some *real love and affection*; this helps her overlook your flaws knowing you accept her as she is.

Do men settle?

Brown women heart-broken resentment from her brother prince's betrayal can be devastating. The rejection of one's mate is traumatically disturbing to the core. Once cheating is discovered (even though some can feel it before they know the facts), they suffer the lost very differently: some people feel emptiness in their gut, the heart functions weakly, lethargy, they grow violent, or darkness covers their thoughts and outlook. They sometime sexually grope after loose women or "pros" for excitement and arousal to mask their inner pain; some become the last poet's description of the "Gash-man" (a male whore) willing to have intercourse, to "fuck," with any and everybody addictively. Too much of this will turn any woman to celibacy, perhaps even lesbianism and in most cases patriarchal hate.

The Brown woman is like every other warm-blooded mammal learning from repeated episodes of pain. When she's been hurt, she remembers it; vowing not to repeat her error of trust.

Ideally, healingly, Brother-Prince needs to come and sweep her up into his strong arms and protect her like the beautiful diamond she feels she is dormant, deep inside. Believe me, there is great power to heal her heart "Mr. Blue Rose" (I'll explain that later).

It is fundamentally vital to have her best be invited out. Showcase her beauty, her flower, publicly, age notwithstanding. Again, sure, her esteem is her own responsibility, but Brother Prince, we are that corny wind beneath her wings. She needs his help to drop healing "love seeds" of charm, friendship, honesty, loyalty, real compliments (holding hands publicly), romance and commitment. To neglect this is to reset a behavior reflux filled with negative bile guarantying a hard and fast reversal backlash when the man, lover or husband least expects it.

We all want to be a gem in some selective eyes of our chosen lover. We all want to find ourselves attracted and attractive to them. We all want to be adored by the "one." We all want to be made to feel like we matter sincerely, naturally, and honestly.

When a woman desires a man, there is no prejudice in his sexual pursuit. The libido does not see color or some social/racial stop sign. It is what it is. "It" wants "it" and that's all there is to it.

In general, the libido knows no creed, status, station, or crest. Ill-cultures that have been indoctrinated through some bias believe system, or negative values can infringe upon fear. It is NOT what neither she nor he need.

Attraction is easily generated by little affection, a lot of fantasy and plain o' hormonal build up. Every woman, young or old, is in envy when a male, young or old, is in pursuit of another woman; pink or brown they share this in common. It's just the way her feminine animal is wired. If she is queen, or bride, she wants and deserves to be the center of her lover's ATTENTION. There is romantic value and stimulation in being pursued and "it" (sex) must be earned. This pursuit, provided she wants you, is a natural turn-on which makes her feel divine and special. This is important to the wellbeing and growth of her spiritual esteem. Here, she feels like a diamond, and she will *feel* included.

Like a moth to flame, it's simple. Show her the flame of real love and she'll flutter around your light for life. When that is absent, women become "confused" about their lover. If he's not "acting" right, or isn't greeting her with a kiss, and treating her with respect, she grows confused and weary. Here is when the man is vulnerable to lose her. This is a dangerous place for him. This can be the opportunity Jody gets your gal and gone.

Henry Morrison Flagler, one of America's first millionaires, had everything to give his wives but because of extreme lack of attention his wife felt instructed by a Ouija-Board to murder him that she might get with a Russian Czar who appeared to pay her more attention. I am NOT suggesting that women are floozies and/or emotionally super-simple, but they are the keepers of love's treasure. It is this reservoir of cupid juice they hold dear to life itself. They will be committed to nurture

you with their drink for eternity—once she
decides.

This is when little girls, 14, 15 & 16
run away with young boys when parents neglect
to show some love; that's real; warm hugs and
affection feels good to her heart—love-seeds;
love-fuel; endorphins. Again, these are
dangerous times when a man, a father or mother
could lose a spouse or young girl to another
bright flame appearance… There is better out
there but if you want the trash…it's your
call.

#

YOUR LACK OF ATTENTION IS THE OTHER ELEPHANT IN THE ROOM

Popular magazines, catalogs, even the beer beverage industry advertisers had better start recognizing the attractiveness in Brown women to be able to sell their products to all audiences—including white men. Brown publishers, prior to the web explosion, such as Ebony, Upscale, EM and Jet magazines started to begin waking up to ornamenting their own ethnic glamour. Oh yes, there was once a time, as late as the late 1970's, when the consideration of Negro models among "Black" publications brought concern to them vs their white model and primary choice.

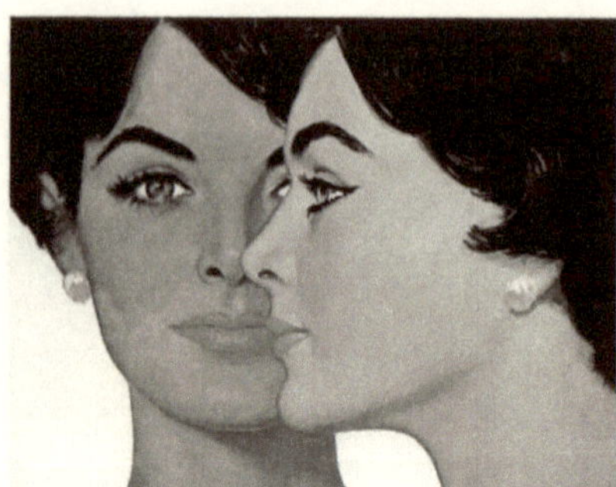

For Dark Skin Problems of Various Degrees

I can remember when print ads in African American magazines were principally white-- really. As a child of late '50's and '60's, I'd often wondered, "Why?" Why, the segregated

mags yet the ads were majority white? I
wondered with the massive explosion of
"Essence Magazine," came the 1980's, for
African American women why so many absent
black models—they were pretty too, to me. I
had hopes for the novelty of the Negro. Below,
is an actual print ad for ARTRA, a skin
lightener, for African women (1940 thru 1970).

Many of the same magazines are doing a
great job, especially with African dress,
cuisines, political diversity, and diverse
cultures. Blacks seem to be adjusting too as
were Whites getting used to Black celebrities-
-slowly. They've begun to discover more opened
doors to white agents, producers and

subscribers excepting of Brown model images. This was, and still is, a breakthrough in the 2,000 millennium.

However, I'm waiting for a time, perhaps someday soon, while sitting in first class within an earshot away, I witness a white male businessperson, who flies frequently, reading and enjoying an old outdated "Jet" magazine and he laments to a flight attendant:

Attendant: Hello sir, would you care for a magazine?
Businessperson: Yes. Do you have this month's Jet?
Attendant: I'm sorry? Jet?
Businessperson: Jet. A magazine...? It's only been around 80 years.
Attendant: Ah, no sir. I'm afraid not. May I offer you something else?
Businessperson: Well, you should have it. It's an iconic American magazine for god's sake. If you want me to continue flying you, I suggest you update your accommodations.

How I long to someday overhear a polite but adamant altercation on a business flight from a white man. It's a bucket-list and of course the next elephant in the room to be confronted.

#

PANGS OF WORTHLESSNESS

So, where does a Brown girl/woman find satisfaction after so much historical and sociological misgivings? There's a lot of unrecognized behind-closed-doors pain where our country once did not care about the social sanity of Black women until the latter 2000's. Unfortunately, and too often, that kind of satisfaction is found at the bottom of some pleasure: ice cream containers, Sara Lee cake boxes, fried fatty foods, spicy soul-food meals, illegal drugs, pregnancy, soap operas, living vicariously through bottom feeding T.V. talk shows, TV court and their flighty advice.

And then there are the esteem killers: living through public assistance, prostitution, hiding behind religious passions and fanaticism or existing like a reclusive hermit has become compensatory fillers. Bottom line to these blights, many Black women need comfort, closure, and help to heal.

Many Jewish women and men, i.e., the children of holocaust victims (Older retirees; elders), still suffer with extreme anti-Semitic paranoia, even though their contemporary Jewish existence have had no interaction with the European Nazis since the 1940's—which I am NOT making light of. Other than the American wanta-be nefarious homeland "Nazis" cults, the younger Jewish population carry the remnant shadows and social yoke their DNA-elders once did. Nonetheless, the osmosis of their handing down these past atrocities during their heinous era, leave scars of genocidal pain that the younger generation vicariously empathize with. Those very challenges carry crossover discrimination from Americans. The 1940's being as fresh as it sounds it is just after their German sterilizing escape. I would imagine this leaves them feeling suspect of any American-Nazis terrorist group.

Clearly one can sympathize with the same sociological behavior effects on African Americans who have been handed down their stories of atrocities for *centuries*—much more than the Nazi decade of the '40's. Blacks are profoundly affected with this lack of social love lost also. Their dehumanizing "love lessness" has grown to render them pangs of the "unlovable."

#

THE BARKING OF BABES

I observe inner cities and listen to the harsh sounds and tones of local Brown ill-parented children's voices. For me, that is always an indication of lacking guidance gone right sometimes and too often gone wrong. Happy or angry sounds are home derived; particularly the male-parent influence or the lack of. "Male love," means when children fear the discipline of papa bear, they fear being seen or ratted-on by other adult bears of their public behavior; it makes a difference more than some single moms will admit. Oh, don't get it twisted, mama bear has an impact. My mother, Seanna Lester, was hell on wheels on my b'hind. However, although he was a lot less violent than she, the disappointment I caused him would haunt me; even though he was slow to raise his hand to me.

The inner city can be Kryptonite for our children. It weakens their desire to be bliss filled. They can't afford to be that happy-go-lucky, puppy catching its tail in the tall grass and all defenses down. But instead, we hear their maladjusted disposition, their negative attitudes and mostly their volatile angst, frustration, and social misery--hence, their defense mechanisms. They consistently seem to seethe with frustration. Boiling just below the skin, they are unfortunately perched and ready to explode with fight.

It doesn't pay to be on the other side of fight mode.

"Say something, I'll slap you into the middle of next week!" These remarks and threats come from home and carry over into the playgrounds, school, workplace, and especially public transportation. Unfortunately, this is where the world observes their perfect home-training and make half-baked bias opinions about "those people."

Sadly, I hear cries of slashing out and I feel resentment from callous emotions jaded by social and economic depravity, being "broke" and without financial stability. I notice how some walk and talk loosely, demonstratively and without discipline; with a deliberate intent to be annoying, loud, and mouthy in public settings; almost groping for a negative effect on their environment. I notice how they just shrug with apathy like a careless hobo; "cuttin' up" and "actin' out" as if crude behavior was a call of the wild or a rite of passage.

The horrible language I commonly hear: "F&#k it!" "Go ahead! Tell my momma." "Whatever!" "It's kool…I can handle dat", "So, what you want me to do about it?", "It happens nigger, awight!", "Life goes on in da' big city", "My brow ain't bent N-word." "What chu lookin' at fool? I don't know you!" "So, you ain't my daddy." I hear these dead-end mantras of negativity mostly from young boys, girls, and their so-called adults daily.

What I don't hear enough of is laughter bursting out of good o' fashion fun coupled by silly pranks; I long to hear that from happy joy filled youngsters. Just good times.

How do you think such behaviour would manifest and swell up in a vulnerable child?

Is this their way of coping with depravity?

Is it because their world lacks so much esteem?

Unlike the Jews, who have unofficially pledged to express their depression, they are healthy to some extent providing their diet of regurgitating and reliving the horrific holocaust past to nullify their pain. This is therapy not obsessive behavior; provided they do not project their indulgence on others. Displacement of blame on others is dangerous and addicting; the hurt one feels from the oppressive years, like a holocaust or slavery period must be sociologically let out to emotionally let go.

Emotional displacing is socially dangerous when blame is cast on someone other than self. E.g., the Confederates still blame the massive deaths of Rebel soldiers on African slaves; a displacement perpetuated into the millennium era. Blame makes the pangs of emotion hurt worst, to fault others other than you. It's not someone's fault that I hurt but the fault of me not owning my hurt that I continue to suffer.

Some Brown people repress their oppress-caused depressions to a social disability; becoming a walking human explosive device; subject to detonation by any sudden agitation much like the inner-city children above we described: "Say something, I said!" "Go 'head, piss me off, hear!?"

It's where those testy "tudes" (attitudes) derived from—the pressure of misdirected blame. Why else would the KKK continue to hood-up or Tiki-down to make their carcinogenic feelings known?

Clearly, it appears they want Blacks to die off. What, with McDonald's Black ads and Republicans votes down Affordable Care Act one would wonder. Racist politicians have signed

up to appeal national HEALTH CARE: a
conservative news network (Fox News) has
signed up, TBN Christian clergy network have
signed up, Martin, Malcolm and Meager
assassins have shut them up, trigger happy
protecting and serving police have signed up,
exonerating IA and judges have signed up, for
profit incarceration facilities have signed
up, our current president (Donald Trump), The
New-England Patriots and their great white
hope quarterback (Tom Brady) didn't sign up.
He told our 44th after a super-bowl win, "No."
'He was too busy that day for a traditional
White-House champion photo.' It's obviously
the fault of the African had they not
convinced slave-traders of their well-deserved
deal of hardship and lack of human-freedom; we
would have never been in this predicament.

Again, mental, and emotional displacement
is dangerous. Real people become explosive
lethal weapons of local destruction.
Unfortunately, and sadly, they are low-esteem
types who often and sadly explode on innocent
bystanders or worst their own dear family
members. It can start with sassy expressions,
but it can easily explode with guns blazing
into an outdoor Vegas crowd.

Anger is like a west coast drought fire.
It escalates and spreads erratically and fast.

Because of these unconscious pangs of worthlessness, their valueless feelings, we experience the proclivity of depression feeling less than human. Their social frustrations run deep, and they experience numbness where they have the dire opiated need to drink, smoke, pop pills or some consume some stimulant that fosters peace or emotional comfort. Once here, they are usually in a funk without reason or cause due to "max'ed out" layers of cultural and social pain. They find themselves simply angry for no real tangible reason they can identify. Pissed off becomes the norm. They react to emotional phantoms, ghost driven negative spirits of the far gone past like the so-called, "civil war."

How is it likely to get free of these feelings?

And yet, we totally, in full irresponsibility, in a society of rules and regulations of dos and don'ts for these culprit inherent inner demons induced by social and political abuse, don't have a freakin' clue as to why we are so freakin' wacked-out and crazy.

Socially displacement gets so bad, the abuser, White or Black racist, set groups up for failure; tricking them to suffer the emotional reverse having the obsessive desire to keep their victims socially arrested gaining nothing but spiritual fatigue.

Its hard work trying to maintain a racist disposition keeping up with oppression updates: the mudslinging politicking, propaganda, hate talk, credit traps, real estate inflation and redlining, and the cost of physically distancing oneself in places one cannot afford to live. The blamer is constantly trying to get rid of the smoking gun, Lady Macbeth cleaning up the blood and covering the trails of tears and evidence is costly work and a 24/7 focus, not to mention the haunt of worry.

It takes enormous amounts of money, energy, and fear to keep racism going successfully. Anything that defiles love is averse to Mother Nature and cannot thrive. This is when our babes bark. It is by our residual spirits we affect them.

Both Pink and Brown children, they're not on board with the hate and separation they feel from us.

#

WITH LIBERTY AND JUSTICE FOR ALL

How do we turn this around for the sake of our health?

It is not a hopeless situation to handle evil. Evil is easy. Most have no idea how powerful prayer is—or the swatting of negative thought when they occur. Prayer the very weapon in the house everyone forgets when they are frozen with fear, or simply meditating frequently enough to self-prove its effectiveness. Prayer is using God and God must/is being used for everything. The problem is we forget these inner powers. We can turn anything around with change, but we must ask the universe, or God, for assistance and help. That's prayer power, i.e., Jedi.

Most of our focus is set to compete (competition). This is not effective when learning to live with one another, or yourself. For example, let's examine an effective thinker vs a competitive thinker. There is no way anyone can know the other guy's prayers, dreams, or the God they serve, but God. One doesn't have to undermine another's assets, attributes, or accomplishments to appear ahead. It's a baseless wish. To do this, is not "winning."

Living in a state of "I have to win" becomes a negative goal. It's stress provoking. This is where the criminal minded, thief or war provocateur is stuck and prone to underhanded efforts.

Take the desperation of pageants, divas and debutantes who fight each other "with attitudes" so they might be scored higher by some phantom-judging party. After a while of this, she only holds herself back.

Trying to be "better than" does not catapult you forward but competes with **yourself**. However, to maximize your horizons, take great steps forward challenging yourself. This is the true exercise. This is the very reason why the racist will always self-destruct following a baseless fight they are "better than." We all must remember that.

Even the South is changing and starting to grope for flat shoes comfort/relaxation).

Hating is too much work. Many red state politicians, businesses and people are trying to do the right thing—get rid of their racist constituents, friends, and family members by flat-out ignoring them. This is NOT easy. It requires prayer and meditation—the force of God to move these obstacles. For me to think every white person is racist is to be a racist. I have met more AMAZING, KIND,

GENEROUS and WONDERFUL white people once I
dropped this baseless profile. And, of course,
I have met the reverse.

I give the South my applause for so much
progress made in such a short period of time--
really. The epidemic made them crazier than
zombies. After such a long oppressive journey
to arrive at this station of civil obedience,
in my life and time, is remarkable. Do they
have work to do yet? Yes, they are NOT
completely out of the woods.

Racism is a lethal cancer and to cure, or
at least to want to, is a milestone to social
health and recovery. This requires the result
of prayer and meditation on all fronts. I am
beginning to feel—just a tad—our country's
effort to be the America our forefather--and
foremothers--constitutionally intended—oh, we
aren't quite there. I am certainly not praying
for an America that once assassinated
presidents, because of their fairness to
ethnic groups and non-white humanity but that
we maintain a liberty driven society without
bias and eek towards a healing.

I am beginning to sense how total freedom
and justice could be all inclusive—not just
those with great wealth but ALL humanity.

**Can I begin to imagine Pinks (South and north)
shopping in Brown areas, without fear, much**

**like African Americans have always shopped in
pink areas?**

And, protested vehemently to do so.
Can I imagine casting talent agents looking
for babies and models of color to promote
commercial demographic without fear of
advertisers worrying about prejudicial
reactions because of the hue of the talent's
skin color, and what that might imply?

Madison Avenue, the avenue of the grand
PR promotional hierarchy and the irrefutable
trend setters of the world, when Madison Ave
(or any advertisement Mecca) says, "Jump," the
world says, "How high?" Can I now imagine
getting the message to Madison Avenue, "…With
liberty and justice for all"? ALL who are
beautiful and photogenic gets an opportunity.

> *But let every man prove his own work,*
> *And then shall he have rejoicing in*
> *Himself alone, and not in another.*
> *{Galatians 6:4}*

#

THE REAL KING OF THE JUNGLE

It is obvious that Europeans, Asians, the Mediterranean and white America are overtly enamored and secretly charmed by the Africanesque and third world in general. Europeans and Israelites are the principal merchandisers of poaching (trading animal parts). They buy and sell all sorts of artifacts from antelope's horns to rare jungle butterflies.

They also love the challenge of the safaris. Here's a life-threatening sport where white people brave through the dark bush and rain forests of African, a land that Africans have lived 338,000 years, day to day, since the beginning of human existence; a thought that I wonder if White superior-conscientious allow them to ponder and accept. It never seems to dawn on White safari hunters or explorers as they so-call "triumph" through the wild "uncharted" frontiers that they're walking in the African's "back yard."

What arrogance they suffer having to make themselves assume the Africans, the original hominid, your "Adamu & Usika" {Eva; Swahili} (Adam and Eve) arguably, have not done these safari expeditions for themselves for countless times--for centuries. In many countries tribal kings were certified by their triumph of killing and capturing a male lion. However, that only happens in a young king's lifetime—in a generation.

Like any hospitable tourist guide, it's their job to recreate an experience for the guest. Like any routine-based administrator, I am sure the African guides are routinely bored to tears like most repetitive worn-out tour guides. I am certain the Lincoln Memorial tour guide hates that song on some days: "Oh beautiful, on spacious skys…" If a jungle happened to be in my back yard, it's highly likely I'm more than aware of what's back there—and how it all behaves after 100's of thousands of years.

To arrogantly think, the indigenous African locals would not know, or be academically unaware, would be like a Brown-American (Bwona; master), leading a group of Eskimos (tourist) to catch a rare polar bear. And, after the "ride" is over and done, as a reward, I pat the Eskimos on their heads for an adventure well done, and an extra gratuity tip with a great comment on TripAdvisor. The joke would be on Bwana (the tourist). An Eskimo guide probably owns a trained polar bear, as a pet. Daily they walk the guests around in glazier circles for hours or days to stage an impossible adventure or a safari. Do you get my point? Safaris need not start with zoos, Disney World, Bush Gardens or Six Flags but with African tourism.

St. Augustine (America's first coast) doesn't live in the first coast Spanish past, but the tourists want to live in their historical present. So, they reenact the past's behaviors of yesteryears for the tourist enjoyment—some days they are bored to tears with their day in and day out excursion displays but a job is a job. The Africans, Eskimos and Spanish re-enactors indigenously live there in their homeland—their trying to make a buck ($)—appearing shocked, surprised, and frightened is part of the silly act for the sake of the tourist's entertainment. But how dare anyone assume they're rural, rustic, and brain-dead native. Can racism make you that stupid? Yes.

An Indian doesn't need to trophy a buffalo, or a Hawaiian doesn't need a tropical fish aquarium, or Alaskans don't need whale ocean sprays showers; nor does Africans necessarily need a zoo when the animals live in his freakin' **backyard** under his human domain. However, white foreigners assume these

Africans are to be guided and led, talked down
to didactically, steered in the right
direction or spiritually saved and sanctified
by European so-called ingenuity. Oh, and
before Darwin, you think the African had a
name for their animals. E.g., (Swahili) Simba
is Lion; (Yoruba) Kiniun; (Zulu) Ibhubesi;
(Xhosa) Ngonyama. Duh.

Have we Americans learned anything about
our Northern grizzly bears, our Florida
alligators, and rattlers? No, not really. But
yes, we have game wardens, and we stay away
from the animals, including pumas and the
cougars…not the "old-hot chicks" but mountain
cats.

HOTTENTOT VENUS

What is up with people who are obsessed and infatuated with year-round tans? Let's face it, Pink/white people look great after a summer tanning—especially richer melon-complexioned Italians, Greeks, Jews, and some melon endowed Scandinavians they adhere beautifully to sun kisses. They look great!

Many Pink women are working hard at

pumping up and firming, their "bustle" (butt; gluteus maximus) and successfully I might add. They'd kill to have a Jalo or a Serrina arse (Irish ass). They purchased ass for cash.

Nevertheless, they might admire with great curiosity the Brown woman derrières but for whatever reason won't express their endearment publicly.   This is what I take issue with. Brown women will gloat about a fresh perm with pride to appear European temporarily until her "kitchen" (back of the neck knotted naps) returns but not whites having an African (Hottentot) rear.

I don't need a research team with special observation skills, and time-line based data, to see that white women are recently growing hormonally back there, or they are purchasing padded undergarments and implanting buttock enhancers, and some look great. Head-turners.

Like Brown women and their perm's and bleaching creams as well as white women and their collagen lips it's not all together authentic in appearance but the idea for more attractiveness to feel better about themselves. The point is well made, it's necessary for the woman to feel beautiful then to look beautiful.

Brown women make it clear they want to be enamored like the Pink woman, but the well-hidden elephant-in-the-room is Pink women's

desire for the Brown women's physical prowess.
They'd kill to sport an ass like Serena
Williams'.

Without direct credit to Brown people,
there are many things they grope at emulating
and recreating in and on themselves: physical
strength, dance moves and rhythm, emotional
strength, spiritual passion, vocal power, and
musical funk; food seasonings, flavors, and
spice alchemy; clean coastal Caribbean waters,
loyalty and respect for eldership and unmoving
faith and love of the Lord. But, for some
ungodly reason, they won't, or can't, for some
peer pressured superiority reasons,
collectively and commercially, admit their
enamoring love for tan looks that relate
abundantly in African melanin.

On the other hand, Brown people have been
desperately in love with European lifestyles;

forever groping for white similarities and approval. This has not changed since Blacks were introduced to European classicism.

Other than Hannibal of North Africa-Carthage who stormed and scorched the Roman Empire captive for 14 years, Africans have not posed any threat to their northern hemispheric counterparts since that time historically. No matter the era or episode of African life in America, have they done anything but try to get along and ally with White-America. They have sought desperately after America to be embraced with acceptance; with great passion: love, envy, and jealousy. Brown people are fascinated by Pink people's undying need to be separated from them. Their reaching-out love efforts are forever rejected. The closer Browns grow toward the Pinks, neighborhood and otherwise, the further and faster the Pinks migrated away.

"For 4800 moons my friend

We've worked like hell for you,

Gave you all my love raised your babies too.

You know that it's true, I love you.

And, I still do. (Poem and song, 1986, NL Lester)

Why do we long to be so included?

Only a fool in love waits for clabbered milk to re-freshen. Brown people seem to sit in broken refrigerator doors waiting for these spoils to return—hoping for a handout, a recognition and/or a regarding nod.

Country western, or any other category of singers, go right to the top of the music charts if they sound remotely as powerful as a Whitney, Aretha, Mariah, Gladys, Mariah etc., or an imitating Adele even who went straight to the top "with a bullet." Even if they cover-sing any of the above artist Brown artist, which is an indication that they're more than enamored with Brown culture then they are willing to admit, they rocket to the top. Except for Michael Bolton, who won't be reminded of his "Black-sound," he has freaked at the question. There's a real phenomenal love-envy passive thing going on here.

But, why is it built on shame...?

Each ethnic group and/or race desire something from the other—I know America now loves Brown men's athletic abilities—that's undeniable true. It's okay because I love linguine, sushi, pastrami, moo shu pork, lobster bisque, shish kebab, chicken Marsala, paella, pizza, and West African peanut butter gravy smothered chicken. America loves to eat cornbread, collards, barbecue, curry chicken and goat, fried chicken southern style, rice-n-peas, jerk chicken, and country ribs. I know many of these items are Black inventions. However, white people prefer to accredit their cuisine gems to Paula Deen and her sons. She knew that White prejudice was NOT going make Brown chefs and cooks popular TV millionaires and the advantage would be all hers by racist default. That's probably how she got in "racial" trouble. She went too far; she simply spoke of the norm from whence she sprang and have benefitted decades since a child.

We all have something wonderful to share, contribute and learn from which makes us all wonderfully interesting and unique. God is no respecter of person: he picks no color to be superior. He/it/she isn't favoring skin-hue to skill. I'm sure of it.

Is the whale of lesser importance than the minnow?

My little children let us not love in Word, neither tongue; but indeed and in truth.

Brown men, there is nothing wrong with worshipping your own. Why not dedicate yourself to "worshipping" your own Brown women in America; other races love theirs. So, you celebrate yours.

Too many CSI forensic TV program are vicariously murdering their own blond beauties every day—a bit too much that I worry for their self-esteem—their lives.

What is this artistic hatred toward white women?

Is its euphemistic anger directed to them because white men, in general, aren't pleased with their recent sexual loyalties? What is the point of killing them off through public entertainment? There are a lot of white women being murdered on TV. Just as you murdered late 18th century South-African Sarah Baartman (Hottentot Venus), an object of white-Frenchmen lust and humiliation, and white

#

HONORED "HOES"

How many renown black goddesses get famously photographed while standing over a subway air vent in Manhattan with the hem of their silk dress being blown up to their neck and she gets posted on colossal billboards in places like Times Square and around the world for decades—making wealth even in her death? Well, there was a time, when Marilyn Monroe made more money dead then she did alive.

And, how did Miss Monroe get such acclaim after such naughty, yet "alleged," promiscuous history with our 36th president of these United States? And yet, she remained an untarnished and celebrated icon with an estate that is still valued over millions of dollars to date? How does that happen?

Historically we are reminded of Marilyn,
but we don't know Duke Ellington's
controversial Coppertone dancer,

Miss Toni Elling

Miss Toni Elling, "Satin Doll," (1953), a beauty that inspired Duke Ellington and Billy Strayhorn to write the very classic piece. She turned up the temperature in the big band speak-easy world

of upscale clubbing. Have you ever heard of
this doll?

How a so-called art-moral and high-minded
country like ours tolerate such strumpet and
brazen behavior from Marilyn, I do declare.
Yet white Americans exclude divas and "divos"
like Toni and Duke from history pages and
required learning? Does this kind of
"cultural-worship" sex goddess mock the
decency and respect for our country's
honorable--not to mention the integrity of our
late-widowed and former first lady Jacqueline
Kennedy Onassis--even in the wake of her
eternal peace Marilyn is historically
perpetuated as the iconic "playmate"?

What dead Brown woman in our history has
remotely come close to this kind of
untouchable white Teflon glorification?

Perhaps it was Dorothy
Dandridge with young Harry Belafonte in the

1954 sensation stage and screen musical,
"Carmen Jones"?

Was it perhaps Diana Ross, once thought
charm school debutante would be the harbinger
of Brown class for our "Negro," or "Colored"
race? She'd be the "great brown hope" to cut
the teeth of our "racial cotillion", but so
far, no cigar.

However though, except for gays, she did
"blow-up" in the 1980's. She crossed many
lines and made some monumental gains, but I
don't remember a "Madison Avenue," "Ross

look."

The gay community had a "crush" on "Miss
Thing Ross." It was universal--especially
Euro-gays. "She was fabulous, darling!!"

She had many back-to-back albums and
innumerable platinum single releases that had
gone through the "Grammy" roof. She was indeed
the "Diva" in good diva company, a candidate

for real competition among most social
circles.

Oprah, for years, had/has that kind of
power and prestige in America—their darling
dear across the board. She's no Ross diva with
unique classic charms and talent but certainly
her legacy is made legitimate honored by her
string of inheriting children.

1 L to R: Ross, Ronda, Chudney, Diana, Tracee & Evan

What a super family dynasty of talent in
tow.

Oprah might be the richest Brown-American
woman in show business to date but she's no
Madison Avenue "Goddess" either--according to
Mad Ave. But to "us," she is the "Grand Diva,"
darling of America and Queen of the media.

Diane however, held her own and gave it a
grand run. Miss Ross was not what Mad-Ave
wanted for white men, at the time, in their

racist purview of white sexual fantasies--
apart from her German ex-husband

Arne Naess, Jr.

For sure, Miss Ross was a record selling
goddess machine for her advertising sponsors.

Names like Diane Carroll, Lena Horne,
Vanessa Williams, and Dorothy Dandridge are
women who culturally epitomized the image of
the Aryan ideal and with great talents
notwithstanding, but Miss Ross was the diva!
They were ladies, professional all, who wanted
to be an excepted, adored and complimented
American. They had it all, except for blond
hair and blue eyes, to which a Halle Berry or
Mary J. Blige could easily oblige themselves,
given their technological eras but thus far
choose not to. After all, anything can be
bought. Again, given their era to the powers

that be, it was about demographic fears. To be white was not a class we Browns could aspire to, only by desire. And, if Negro women got too close to "whitedom"—like publicly kissing a cinematic prince--there was commentary, dropped sales and applied discomforts of tension put her way.

These ladies above were found to be socially and acceptably light skin to which Whites could tolerate or accept the mulatto starlet a lot easier. They were near ordinary people to put it frankly.

Obviously, these ladies were well applauded and worthy dolls of distinction in anyone's view. They made America money also but never were they the ordain breath taking goddesses and blue-blooded capitalist hope to bring home to meet mom (See the movie, "Human Stain" starring Anthony Hopkins {who plays a mulatto black man & Nicole Kidman.)

So again, where do Brown men factor into these issues?

Are they out of touch or unaware of these racial blights, divides and silent skin color wars Brown women suffer? Or are Brown men too stymied by the Hefner air-brush photo-shopped center folds and Sports Illustrated swing wear to smell the brewing coffee and sizzling bacon of propaganda frying in their own kitchens?

Can we help change these inordinate cultural stagnations?

If not, how do we get up to speed and lift to date our candidacies for "Goddessdom"? When do we pass down a constant perpetuated pageantry of Bourgeois debutantes and cotillions among our offspring? What is happening to our Black-professional parents and their "Jack & Jill" children's rite of passage?

The Brown woman, like any women, feels the same passions: to be regarded as beautiful, adored and perhaps a "diva" candidate—it's any young girl's dream—at least to be in the running; it's their nature to be pretty. Brown women arguably do not want to be anybody's throw-back girl—by Pink men or Brown men—she's known enough disappointments from Brother Prince by default of traumatic duress: slavery, peonage, prison absence, ghetto life, pimped and economically disproportioned.

I stand firm on the theory that these measures of social ills have affected our lack of true sense of self. The lack that will erode self-esteem: I am, I am empowered, and I

have inner decisive strength. This ongoing
social dynamic of ornate pretentions of civil
acceptance by legislation, law and not by the
heart of fellow mankind will in no way show
anything less than angry hard faces filled
with attitudinal feelings where Brown people
stand outside the judgment of their
discriminating obstructions blaming each other
for their surroundings. Hence, this might be
the cause of gang banging's, Black on Black
crime, drive by shootings and public
disobedience.

Why is all of this happening to Brown women—to us all?

How does she raise healthy children in this environment?

Why is this curse lingering among us so?

I can't help but imagine the shadows of
slavery still haunting us in dormancy given
these ongoing negative stimulants that reoccur
over and over; somehow in the annals and
archives of our deep unconscious minds, we are
like post-war vets who still suffer
insurmountable trauma trying to forget, hide
our heads in the gospel sand, or pretend "it"
never happened as we stare in the mirror at
our hair perms and processes.

Trauma like this never just goes away. Low self-esteem or worthless feelings are intrinsic pain that need closure. It's never going to happen until the "hoes" are less honored than the true divas should be. These hoes are honored in every magazine: whether they've rocked bottom, driven by debauchery or crown by royalty they still make the magazine; the "honored hoe" is a cancer growing among everybody soul because we are losing our sense of right and wrong.

#

THEIR FINGER, BLUE AND BLOOD PRINTS

There is something yet emotionally afoot and
without closure in African American's blood
prints—our DNA memory that is. There is
something hidden that isn't ready to reveal
itself; some spiritual matrix that is still
hereditarily inherent in our blood. Through
consciousness and spiritual memories, I
speculate perhaps it's waiting to spring. It
is being genetically handed down through blood
samplings. And maybe it's trying to "purify"
itself for the right time and event.

I think we carry these "blood-blueprints"
of our ancestors in the deep trenches and
molecules of our genomes (genes inside a cell)
and chromosomes (Threadlike acid and protein
coding inside cells). DNA (Deoxyribonucleic
Acid), according to proven data, can transfer
intelligent capabilities but not intellectual
quotient (I.Q. or knowledge), or what's been
learned by the parent donor. I submit that the
capacity for retention and learning can be
duplicated in our offspring and in many cases
enhanced. I believe, like mental capability
inherited, we can consciously transpose
cultural memory linearly. For example, all the

forced cross breeding of former slaves carries with the traits of both species along with their resentment of being white or black. Human studding practices and house-nanny rape have left their offspring with trust issues toward white men. Resentful slave trade has perhaps resulted in some angry spiritual manifestation in need of closure through revenge lingering yet in black people's blood. Where white DNA hate derives from, I am yet puzzled, perplexed and without a solid theory *(See, The Forbidden Memory, Amazon, 2020)*. I don't know why they are angry—is its displaced guilt?

Dr. Oz solidly believes "Black people suffer high-blood pressure as result of their crossing the Atlantic through high stress and duress" that remains with us even though 1619 has passed. Could these blood samplings be seeking some predisposition outcome to avenge their bygone blight; handed down in our blood-prints?

Let's face it, many Brown people are angry and for good reason. We/they try to nullify it in church by singing at the top of their lungs, praising hard and long, and shouting it off vehemently to temporarily sooth their souls but it's still their anger; ever present waiting to burst.

What did happen to these unresolved feelings Brown ancestors repressed away?

Are they any different than a duped, "played" and forsaken "Carrie" from the supernatural horror movie? Are there similarities in us like that of the Hulk looking to physically explode? Could perhaps those iconic Comicon-stories be based on African research and some latent truth? After all, it is quite intriguing that superheroes grow great powers once threatened or angered. I believe some spiritual catharsis happened in the darken stench filled bowels of those slave ships—an inner power and a massive unforgiving strength innately grew in their blood.

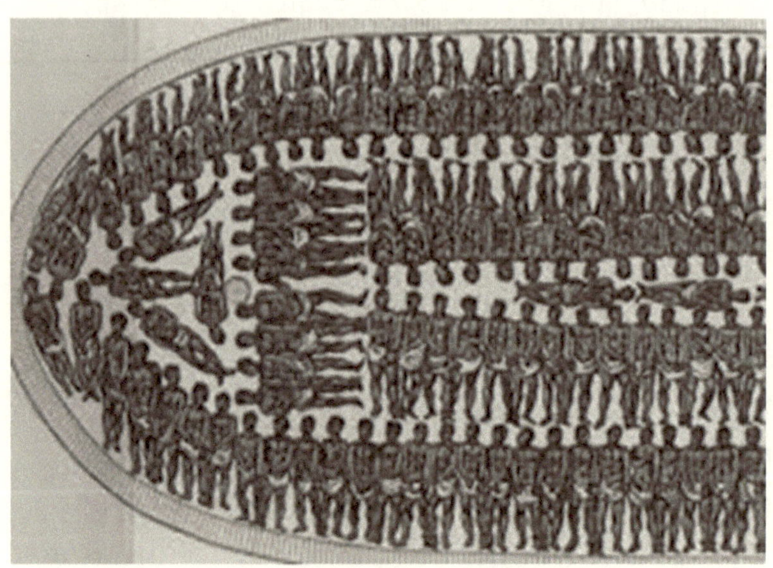

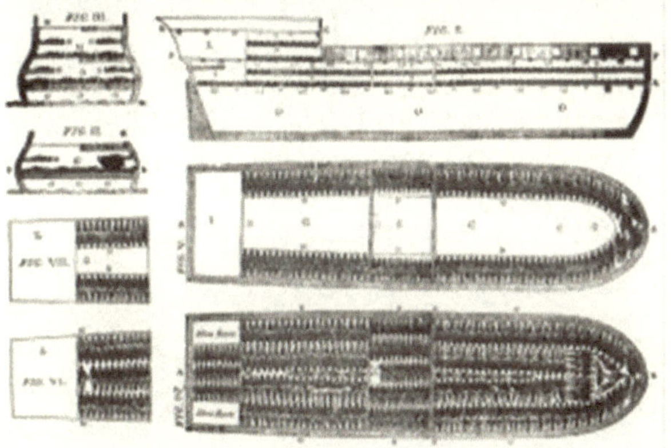

Do these passions just go away with the death of victims, or do they continue to rise to set wrongs right?

The paranormal experts stand by that theory that apparitions are still here trying to settle wrong doings. They are called "imprints." It is very much a ghost theory from every occult investigator I've met, "They have not passed on because of wrongs that need to be set correct."

Poltergeists are Native-American ghost resurrected because of burial disrespect;

excavated to be replaced by "proper" or more civilized Catholics burials and/or for real estate innovations causing a "restlessness" in the grounds beneath.

Are these feelings still inherently in us even though they might be hundreds of years old and dissipated? I say, yes.

As a watcher (observer of people and their inner spirits), I see Brown people when I'm out and about. I sense their unsettled disclosure. I see and feel their feverish attitudes of angst and dissatisfaction and it appears always ready to explode; just below their thin-skin surface; more than often waiting for an initiation or an invitation to open a can of whup-ass. I hear it in their explosive voices too often; taken out on their children, sadly. I lament hearing that because, yet another generation of angry cocoons are being spun. I want so desperately to say something, but I never know how to approach them without getting in their business. Perhaps, I'm just cowardly afraid like most people when amid a rabid human snarling at their own pains of depravity.

#

WE'LL TALK ONLY TO AND WITH OSCEOLA.

Look at the "light skinned" African Americans contingent spread throughout these United States and all around the world. There is miscegenation (mixed races) as far as the eye can see. Clearly, given the practice of racism, then and now, with so MANY light-skinned Brown people, we can see where rampant rape has had its unchecked practice, and I would imagine a great deal of consensual agreements. There's been a tremendous amount of non-consensual sex being bartered behind closed barn doors and bushes.

        The documentation of photographs from the
late 19ᵗʰ century, pre-civil war and even
before then, you can visually measure the
blood influence of mixed marriages, or
"violated" victims, dating back some two
centuries ago by skin tone alone.

                                        You can tract and
find this evidence everywhere. Africans had
been repeatedly abused with regularity and no
laws in place to protect them. There are many
scientific telltale signs of miscegenation.
But the common-sense, sure shot identifying
fact of DNA exchange is within the question:
Are there light-skinned mulattoes found among
Nigerians, Congo, Sudan, Ivory Coast, Senegal,
or Ghanaians? Since Ghana was one of the
center regions where the River Niger ran
through, whence slaves were extracted
principally from Africa's West Coast no
mulattoes were recorded there? It was their
arrival in the states where later light-
skinned children began to spring up.

The Senegalese principally spoke French
and has been a province of France for
Centuries—hence ½ breeds, mulattoes, dark vs
light skin, caste systems and linguistic
French influence developed among the Africans
there.

And, if you socially track Negro family
trees you will also find where we have
accepted our miscegenation as a crowning or

blossoming diversity to our "Bouquet" lot. Browns have endearingly referred to our race as the Negro, "Niggra," Colored, Blacks, Afro-Americans and now African American or to coin my dad, Steve Lester, "The Bouquet Race." There are regional hubs throughout America where these hue distinctions are prevalent: ATL, New Orleans, Savannah, Harlem, Philly, Chicago and especially our nation's capital where there's been a great deal of "cross flesh-colonizing" in ye ole district. I am not talking about recent interracial coupling since the 1960's with hippy free love but century old widespread behind closed door activity. There are a myriad of skin shades and colors due partially to antebellum (post-war) sexual violations.

Oddly, in my growing up in Trenton, NJ, Colored people applaud this light-skinned outcome without prejudice for reasons of blood line survival. Civil Rights Activist, **Rev. Joseph Lowery**

boldly during the benediction of President
Obama's 1st inauguration, 2008, said:

*"Lord, in the memory of all the saints who
from their labors rest, and in the joy of a
new beginning, we ask you to help us work for
that day when blacks will not be asked to get
in back, when brown can stick around...when
yellow will be mellow...when the red man can
get ahead, man; and when white will embrace
what is right. That all those who do justice
and love mercy say Amen."*

He made a humorous analogy to an age old
oppressive behind the curtain atrocity; a
caste system initiated by American supremacy
and human slavery. Mind you, the rhyme was bit
different back in the day. Perhaps the good
reverend augmented it politically and
appropriately given the event and changed the
phrasing. But, traditionally, among Black
folk, it went more like: "If you black get
back. If your brown stick around. If you

yellow, you mellow and if you're white you all
right"—or some order like that. What would
make a 91-year-old pastor have nerve enough to
imply such Black coding and chance such an
outrage statement like this during a
historical and monumental racial turn over in
American history; to which MANY whites raged
while it happened not remotely receiving the
wisdom in his words. I remember seeing
President Obama slightly chuckling with
amusement. Fox News, however, which swore not
to cover the inauguration, decided to attack
this innuendo—no doubt some "House Negro"
pulled their coat. Why is there no regard for
such an acclaim elder (Rev Lowery) of civil
rights in our community?

2 Rev. Lowery 2nd from left

An icon of a man (Rev. Lowery, with
glasses, left of Martin) who has fought with
life threatening protest for rights to be
delivered for all mankind; in a country that
goes to war for freedom and swears to die for
that very cause yet Negros who now live
emancipated by law gets no civil respect.

Andrew Jackson tricked millions of
"Seminole" Indians into Fort Marion in St.
Augustine, where they had posed a truce to
settle the war among Indians and white
settlers but were really duped, tricked and
entrapped. The Seminoles along with Osceola, a

Chief Osceola by George Catlin ca. 1838

half white man
and his Indian followers, (he was Creek, Scot
Irish and English mixed) --the White-Americans
soldiers were only willing to negotiate with
him—the Noles' leader, to surrender and later
put them to death—via genocide.

Fortunately, many got away and like many
Indian tribes they too mixed among Africans to

189

survive their blood lines, hence the name Semi
(half) nole--Seminole.

This is a delicately mortifying but very
much the truth about early White Americans
civil principals.

But like their own Blood-prints they too
must become aware of their own purification
and that does not mean color. Sure, these are
harsh facts. I don't know how to approach them
more gingerly. It's an issue that lives yet
today that we must all face for the sake of
some kind of "human-closure." Something,
unfortunately, many republicans, namely Ron
DeSantis, fear to do by eradicating these
facts from our school libraries and Florida
curriculum. To go forward with these lies, is
to build yet another house of cards that
doesn't strengthen this nation but add to its
fragile gangster mindedness that gropes to
control resources for their own racist
interest and weaken our constitutional base.
Osceola was not an Indian leader among the
Creeks but a figment of white-American
prejudice and racist need to feel superior,
rendering him an inferior soul.

#

SMOKEY ROBINSON'S BLOOD IS TALKING: LIGHT-SKINNED PRINCE

Many Brown people have come to fancy some of their light-skinned features as a romantic and crowning. Remember: "If you're Brown, stick around…?

Our so-called colorful-matrix is an encroachment of oppressive and historical violations—not all naturally, but most. It's an embarrassing truth since the beginning of the African's time in North America; Brown women have been regretfully and repeatedly abused along with off-the-criminal-record absence of law, or wherewithal to prosecute.

During the Louisiana French influence, and after, the French bourgeoisie would abduct or purchase mixed baby girls especially, to rear them as professional concubines better known as "Octoroons" or "Quadroons," i.e., escorts, prostitutes, bred for brothel use.

These considered bastard children who
were mixed with four to eight races gave
purpose to life by exploitation of their
flesh. They'd pick only the half white, or
partially so, and black females to rear them
for this ill-repute occupation during the 17th

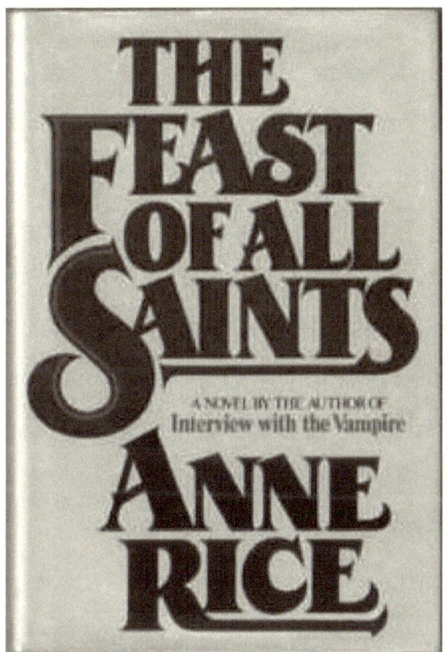

States.

[14]This novel is about the <u>gens de couleur libres</u>, or <u>free people of colour</u>, who lived in <u>New Orleans</u> before the <u>Civil War</u>. The gens de couleur libres were the descendants of European settlers of Louisiana, particularly the French and Spanish and people of African descent. It was a common practice for the early Caucasian settlers to free their children by their slave mistresses. Their mistresses, however, were not all enslaved, some were free women of colour whose families had been free for several generations. The novel takes place in the 1840s, at which time there was a large population of free people of colour living in New Orleans.

The story centers on Marcel, a young man who has one white parent and one parent who is half white and half black. His mother, Cecile, is the mistress of Philippe Ferronaire, a rich French <u>plantation</u> owner. Cecile has borne Ferronaire two children, Marcel and his sister Marie. Marie is very light skinned and able to pass as white, but Marcel, who is blonde and blue eyed, but with ethnic hair and darker skin, cannot.

---

[14] Publisher: Simon & Schuster, 1979; Wikipedia 2015

Admirably, Mulatto types then were regarded as "light-skinned" beauties, "high yellow" and "red bone." These mulattos are still marveled as beauty symbols in many brown communities yet—especially rap videos and hair product models—not the station or class necessarily but simply the look of skin fairness and keener features.

It has been, and still is, the ambition of many Brown men and a priority of many Brown families, prior to and during the 20th century, to be free, educated and marry a "light-skinned" woman with "good hair" (Straighter hair; or at least broader curls that aren't kinky). Anything Brown that principally resembled the features of the Caucasoid (whites) is/was readily acceptable ("…They were all right," Rev. John Lowery), the opposite being the obvious disdained and rejected ("If you Black, get back; Brown, stick around," sorta'). These stigmatic, canonized standards were advocated and welcomed with serious acceptance; vehemently appreciated by Brown women and men. They abhorred the idea of naps or an untrimmed "kitchen" (knots on the back of the neck) as it were. These ideals remain and maintain to this day in many cultures unfortunately.

A "light-skinned beauty" was, (Bill and
Camille) and is, the princess menagerie

of most Brown neighborhoods and family prime.

(Frederick Douglas & wife Helen Pitts) Every
prospering and decent Brown man should seek

one for their successful completion,

(Mr. & Mrs. Nat King Cole) especially
Brown professional men: lawyers, physicians,
morticians, and famous performers

(The late Don Cornelius and wife
Victoria) and clergy leaders as well.

It was, and still is, a paramount practice among Brown families even during these modern times sadly to bring home a light-skinned promise for marriage.

Figure 3-Cleveland, Cora, Estina and Jovita

(Mr. & Mrs. Paul Robeson, wife, son & his family above) Yes, I had one too (Above Estina C. Baker, 1985). It was a promise-land ideal, the path to success and happiness. And, then I grew up.

(Noble Lee & Lena Annette, 2011) It is a stretchy theory, but we are working against

the odds of a slow-moving evolution, an
evolution that is playing out, not in the
physical realm but through the years of
conditioned influences that we carry in our
genes, our DNA trying to escape this painful
color burden. This is the blueprint not only
of our physical manifestation but of our
spirit and possibly of our souls.

We are so behest by this looming topic we
fail to fall before God and thank him for whom
we are and let the power of that over-shadow
any force that might advocate the reverse or
otherwise. We must allow and be willing to
behold the beauty of self-inside so that it
may so shine with brilliance:

Smokey Robinson may have been "beautifully
light-skin" but even he realized the rose-
colored prism lens he was shamed into seeing
himself a far from being African and
beautiful.

Malcolm X said, "Who taught you to hate
your lips, the size of your nose, color of
your skin, texture of your hair and to hate
each other so that you don't have to be around
each other?!?"

#

ENVIRONMENT RULES!

I believe we genetically seek out hardship in
one fashion or another to live out our
inherited learned social patterns; our natural
design and purpose based on our available
consciousness, recorded upon our "blood
prints" (DNA). For example, if you were raised
wealthy there is a strong likelihood such
things like lifestyles, political influences
and habits will intrinsically manifest or
evolve into learned destinies.

When we grow from or hail from anarchy
and war worn events, adulatory, crime and
murder, urban property destruction, poverty
and filth, welfare dependencies and
prejudicial narrow-minded viewpoints, we tend
to move toward or favor these environments as
it kicks hard in our blood for manifestation
in our reality. We are looking for
manifestation and destiny outlet to which we
are familiar—positives and negatives. We live
out what we've learned or come to know. When
these "learned things" are not fulfilled as
our primary mind has deemed them "real" from
environmental influences, we feel out of
sorts, out of our element and useless with

need to go back to our honed "hood" as it were.

Opulence ceases to "be real" to our self if there is no "ghetto" to refer to or live in. People have turned mansions into ghetto existence.

No one needs a trailer park home or a ghetto nor a "to die for" Malibu ocean glass view bungalow. However, we need to be what we were or know or most familiar with.

Like pigeons, we tend to hone back to the nest of our physical and spiritual origin hence the same for human upbringing; unless we grow aware of our condition to grow away from it for improvement. We all fly back "home"; whatever or whatever that home may have been we desire to go home to roost.

***

Similarly, we are born inherently with genes that combat and ward off specific diseases. The human body expects to be confronted at some point in time with a bio-enemy encroachment of sorts. For example, antibodies passed down through DNA ward off foreign physical intrusions it has known through some other pathogenic host. The body's auto-immune defense mechanisms will seek the disease directly or vicariously just so it can live out the purpose of its existence—measles, shingles. It wants to do what it's been designed to do—to seek and destroy foreign bodies.

The same with hundreds of years of unending duress, stress, oppression, separated families due to slave trade, being swapped, obstructing indigenous languages and cultures, cussin' and fussin' and outlawing native cultures, thwarting gender romantic communication and outlet, personal dignity and privacy do we live out the blood-prints sat before us in origin. These blocked "intrinsic things" have reformed another dynamic which has led us innately to be racially divided and fundamentally uncomfortable. To remedy these atrocities, we implement legalities beseeched by law. civil rights, voting rights, a complete education, etc. These laws may legally protect us against suspecting, faithless and doubtful politics where we are forced to socially unite and stand together is nothing less than pretentiousness and pitied acceptance. This doesn't eradicate biases or fill the heart with acceptance or help the segregated heart to feel welcome, included or approve. This does not improve our self-worth but diminishes it.

Are we to continue to play out a life our oppressors have moulded for us after hundreds of years of slavery, political rejection, civil war animosity and confederate blame?

Confederate flags fly, red-necks and cracker mentality proudly continue to aggrandize in these modern times looking to go back home to where they hail from and are more familiar with--same honing principal.

Does Negro DNA desire yet to be slaves?

Do White racist-Americans desire yet to master, use and abuse "slaves?"

There is a far greater unconscious influence over our lives than racism and financial depravity: it is the destructive environment we can't seem to let go and get free of in ourselves. Don't let the ghetto environment rule you but you rule it simply by being aware that your "programming" comes from ONLY you and NEVER the oppressor ultimately.

#

SO-CALLED DIFFERENCES

How is it we hear music differently than
others: White music or Black music. Having
grown up and in the same environment for 450
years how did racism augment our ears? I get
that Greek music is different from German
music but when you put the two cultures
together in the same environment for the same
length of time (450 years) I would imagine
some commonality would evolve, some
development or cross-pollination would
naturally occur. How did immigrant Jewish
producers of the 1950's become so adept to
Colored people's doo-wop music, as well as
Negro innovative big band (Duke Ellington, Cab
Calloway, and Count Basie) sound and solo jazz
bands (Dizzy Gillespie) in the early 1960's
until the 1990's (Miles Davis) and along
followed fusion jazz (Herbie Hancock and
Santana)? Were they redlined to coexist with
Blacks they had no other choice? Many Whites
then could not admit to Blacks their musical
joy, in America, so they let Jewish producers
and retailers solicit their interest and
business not having to associate and be
embarrassed with contact of Negros; but the

next lower-class citizens, Jews, could. Ray Charles was one of the first to own his master recordings to the Jews' disappointment. This was a shock because white-discriminated Jews were relegated to exploit Black talent as a means of wealth.

How do Blacks get over this mistreatment to trust white-America?

Not just mistreatment but the deep trauma of color indignation and human depravation do we ask the above question. Just to be Harriet Tubman alone having to liberate Nigras through the shadows of the South (Maryland and Virginia), to exodus them far beyond the "North" for absolute freedom, it was Canada where there were no laws implemented, giving bounty hunters the right to return "slaves" found as far north as NY state and Canada line, was an immeasurable task. This is a mortifying horror no God-fearing man or woman can deny.

Congress passed a bill in 1850, "The Fugitive Slave Law," allowing anyone capable to round up Nigra runaways for cash. Social degenerates and heartless slackers made a career of this—and to think for some the

Confederate Flags fly high in their front lawns today honoring such bounty.

Confederate pride?

This is evil itself boldly bragging. How is that done and to wear a war time medal at the same time? —it's despicable. Again, Harriet Tubman was forced to seek freedom in Canada—the north was no better. How does the soul of Africans Blood-prints erase these intrinsic horrific recordings that we might find relief from such anguish?

Perhaps reparation?

The national Veteran Hospital is the perfect testament of war time atrocities and illness fallen upon our soldiers: wounded, captured or traumatized by heinous torture or killings, collateral murder, and hardship death. They deserve reparation for their service: help, patience, and sympathetic care to work away these issues and failed circumstances around healthcare. Veterans are being undermined for personal gain, hospital collusion and inside greed of Federal money. Well, Niggers, Coons, Negras, Negros, Colored people, Blacks or African Americans have never received any country driven counseling and insistence on oppressed slavery for mental and emotional repair, but they too are being undermined for personal gain, political collusion and greed of Federal monies, reparation notwithstanding.

In 1963, President Kennedy sent The National Reserves to secure one little girl to an elementary school by his order. This is not therapy for ex-slaves, hangings, castrations, and child abductions. The FBI goes to war with any inside homeland obstructionist or anti-American who treasons or deface our laws and civil liberties. If one molester crosses a state line, the FBI is on the hunt—Silver Alert! Let our Feds do the same for haters who oppress Brown-American citizens with hurt, harm or peonage against the laws of our land—go Gold Alert!! Make it homeland war! The Taliban, Al Qaeda, ISIS or the KKK should all be the same to National security. You want a war? Well, fight like hell against racist behavior in our own country that we might continue to STAND for peace and good will toward ALL men and women. Enough is enough.

#

SO-CALLED RELIGION DIFFERENCES

How is it you cry silently in service but shout happy in church?

How is it some talk to God before a meal and others try not to talk to each other during?

Why is it some knock the hell out of their children when they sass, and others call for time-outs?

It's not unlikely to believe our psyche routinely and actually expects to be confronted with these above questions, ills and issues: "You're gonna git a good whoppings," "She gotta beatin'," "I'ma whoop yoh ass til it rope like okra." "I'ma slap you into the middle of next week!" All these examples of verbal abuse I heard as a child from my parents and other families; depending on their religious depth and southern commitment to child-rearing, I received most of those above threats, if not all of them. I like to refer to such abuse as bygone slave-discipline.

When will the Browns be allowed to therapeutically vent, or heal, from these deeply rooted oppressive blood-prints of behaviors, where they now routinely and expect "abusive" corporal punishment assisted by belt buckles, braided switches, leather blade straps, wooden paddles, and extension cords to offer results?

Do we even regard this "whupin'" as a level of emotional sickness?

No. It was good enough for massa' (slave trader) to "break our spirit" or "chastise us good." It's unconsciously favorable enough to carry the learned behavior on. "If it broke that Negro's bad-ass spirit, it's good enough in my house."

No. Again, it's another blood-print: there is nothing "good" about an "ass-whupin'"; particularly Massa's admonishing style of punishment that we depraved souls continue to perpetuate. It didn't work then, and it isn't today. These POWERFUL and unbreakable spirits just get meaner.

We must remember that massa wasn't "breaking someone" he cared about or love dearly he was training livestock property, coping with a subhuman or an animal-man--to his dreadful fear.

Psychiatric and psychologist call this a festering state of repression and denial that we take abuse out on ourselves and call it good child-rearing.

Sociologist Dr. Joy DeGruy-Leary, PhD calls it "Post Traumatic Slavery" where both abused slave and abusive master suffer a "cognitive dissonance" where the psyche makes up an emotional excuse to disenfranchise another human and deprive them their natural freedoms with any obstruction necessary to belittle them. They suffer from the same syndrome, but the slave contributes to his own pain by means of self-perpetuating these blights not knowing it is not a normal behavior. "Ima whup yo' ass good heah?"

When we don't vent personally or communally, we are in jeopardy of mental illness and emotional breakdowns and communal mayhem. Abuse of any type, especially slavery, will erode the soul of its host's precious self esteem and worth. This is the very topic of Moses' biblical story— "Let my people go…" Clearly, God wanted freedom for all kind. These actions cause the host to grow physically unsightly, or ugly, outside itself.

Physical beatings are a catharsis to these dark depressing ends. It's a miracle Negros in America have not gone stock raving mad from these handed down standardized punishments. It's a wonder we are not ranting lunatics and out of our minds with resentment.

To have suffered extreme brutality, and still,
they rise despite their traumas,

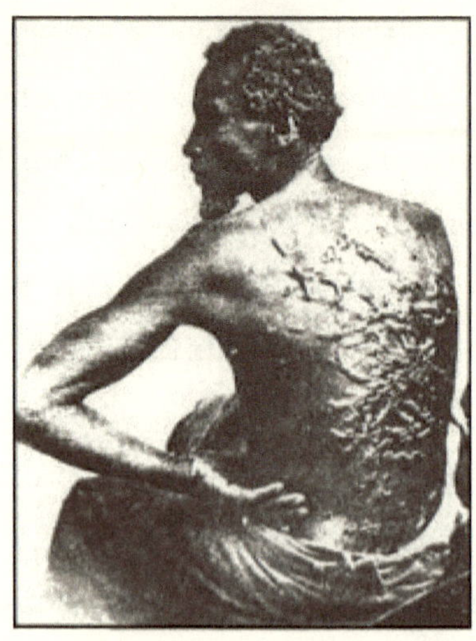

it's a wonder we're not killing, looting, and
deceiving one another even more than we have,
or are we? We are completely out of our
element trying to mask these underpinnings
with societal normality—Browns are still angry
at everything: white people, their "own kind,"
the government, the south, the north also, the
bank, jobs, lacking income and industry. We
are in denial of our anger toward the church
to which we equally fear. We hate the dope
pusher because we need him more than we'd
like—needing him so much and so often; we
love/loathe him.

Many Browns have healed but too many are
yet in need of help. What do you think you're
looking at in a depraved ghetto neighborhood—
the manifestation of anger—self-directed.

Martin Luther King, Jr. was right given the Brown circumstance. Violence would have literally released a Hulk-like monster in us. This is what Malcolm didn't understand about non-violent tactics. White politicians feared the monster-Frankenstein they had created. Martin knew whites had no cause to EXPLODE in anger. They had been the benefactors of Black oppression. Therefore, reporters repeatedly asked the question incessantly, unceasingly, "Does Elijah Muhammad teach violence?" "Does he hate the white-man?" Therefore, Malcolm was bewildered by their lack of intelligence that they never heard his clearly stated reply, "The Honorable Elijah Muhammad has never taught his people violence." It wasn't what the Muslims were doing as much as it was White people's inability to control their political driven fear they were in denial of. Our blood-pressure epidemic was telling them the "Hulk" in the Brown people was coming. White people's hate toward Black people is really their fear in denial. White bullies are just a small minority of killer-bees dispatched to invoke fear for the "scaredy-fat cats" watching from the hill.

There are still Brown fallen soldiers, shell shocked and nullified by institutionalized depravity. Like VA soldiers

after only a few years, they are never quite
right (See movie: "The American Sniper"); a
healing progress must take place for master as
well as former slave cultures otherwise we
will continue to chase our broken tails madly
and sociologically. This must commence
yesterday. We need therapy and we need closure
now. Like mass shootings from white angry
children toward innocent white students, this
has caused a rage in white "high-schoolers"
across the nation. It is the same effect of
fatal abuse that causes rage and push-back.
Thus, the same with Black Lives Matter
movements, they wish the abuse to STOP!!

Most of our African purity and continent
traditions have been annihilated culturally,

erased and what's worst, misrepresented with
consistent apathy and pathetic insult and
disgust. Conservatives don't want to talk
about their painful guilt, liberals don't know
how to TED, or talk about it, for fear of
offending African Americans and wound up
feeling alone flash dancing somewhere or
rallying by themselves—holding the bag as it
were because Brown people don't trust their
color.

Dr. Marcus Garvey, PhD, and his Negros
exodus back to Africa was undermined and
dismissed as fantasy, a cartoon, and a joke of
incompetence.

Because of our deep-rooted illness of
worthlessness having been "broken" and/or
beaten into submission, we laughed at Dr.
Garvey more than Whites ridiculed his effort
at the time. Marcus

simply advocated if you hate me so then let me

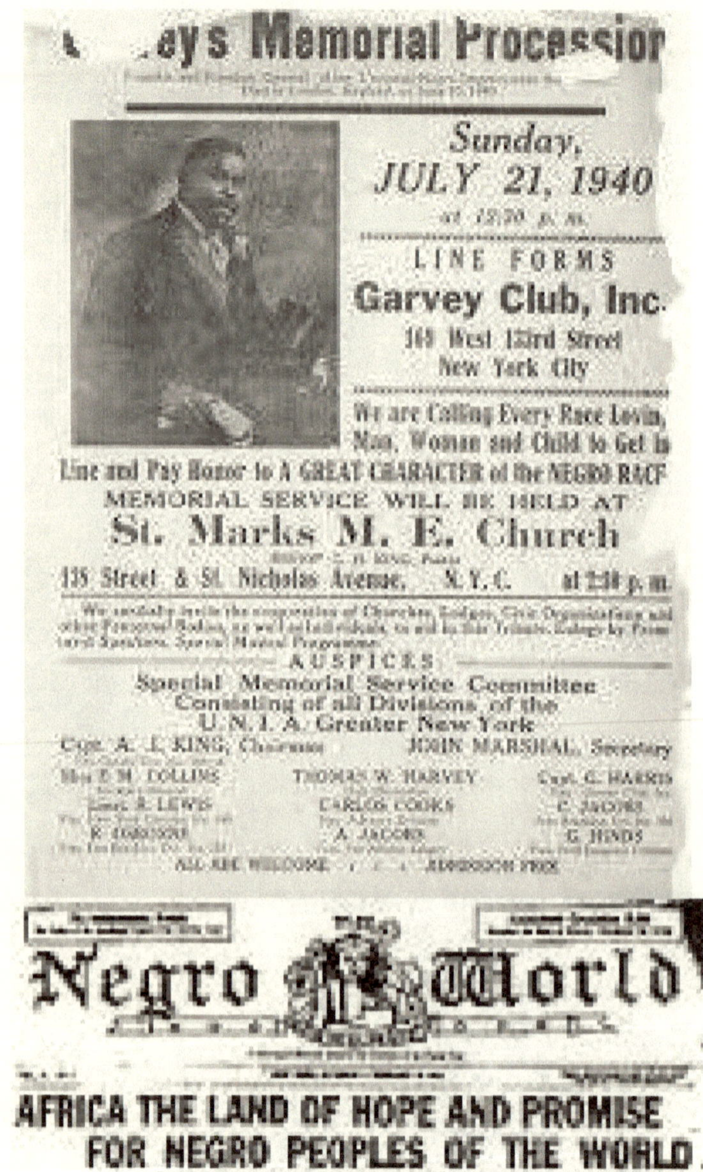

go—go back home.

(LOL) "The foolish idea of going back to Africa in an ocean liner full of jungle bunnies" was rendered insipid by Blacks, Browns and Whites. His news critics shamed him, "Such silliness." Browns went along and shared in the ridicule as an act of expressing commonality with whites in desperate hope of feeling included.

The primary reasons for those who ridiculed their fellow Africans, unfortunately, have never experienced the dignity, social training, cultural heritage, and like depraved animals, they know only their master's mentality—trying to suck-up. They agreed and saw themselves as nothing more than "Jungle bunnies" sadly. They were intellectually without a functional clue and knowledge that they ever needed such things as freedom—just their former master's approval.

I see annihilation and madness in our urban streets of the inner cities, along with self-destruction and genocide they not quite understanding just why we're in this negative funk and spiritual pain as Blacks assist in fueling it with angry sounding music, wearing debilitating clothes, attacking those who would lend a hand of advice or wisdom. There are fights and killing for no reason, drugs that happen to conveniently "fall" into Brown neighborhoods. Brown men, and women of late, arrogantly thinking that jail time is a personal challenge: "I can do 5 easy, man!" College is a waste of time. Many provoke diabetes with improper diets. A lot of Brown people are losing their faith and debunking the church as hustling-pimps who collect the poor people's 10% off the gross top.

There has been NO closure for the African to properly heal except for some churches and social programs where their belief system in Christ and each other are exercised with consistency. Many teach an innate nature of cornucopia, there is plenty that is not always capitalized on.

No one highlights and advocates louder than Brown people how "You can't beat God giving." Nothing compares to this focus of faith that God is and has blessed them with survival.

Yet, those who are lost and without in the inner-city wastelands, are walking around in circles dazed--especially the growing numbers of homeless. Some Brown people follow any trend that flashes like glitter looking forward to nothing but death.

Their bellowing tides of self-destruction roars with crashing waves where no beacon of light from cultural lighthouses searching to

guide them home to shore has evolved. However,
it is my belief, Jesus has provided that
light. I cower to imagine our country without
His light of love. In my opinion, it is not
the church lethargy and practices that
provides that light but the exercise of
controlling our thoughts with unfailing doubt
in them and taking the responsibility of our
desires and let that effort be in Jesus' name.

Africans need this light to be led back
to the purity of their original peace, not
necessarily their original place which long
dissipated but to a place of inclusion and
self-providing restitution.

Africans were once a loving people and
that still lives in their blood—prints. Any
tightly knitted community or church or even
gangs are evidence of that fact. It is this, I
do believe, that will heal the lack of love
relations, families, and marriages in our
communities. This goes for whites and blacks
that we might overcome our *so-called
differences* and cognitive dissonance.

> *Who can find a virtuous wife?*
> *For her worth is far above rubies.*
> *…She makes tapestry for herself; her*
> *Clothing is fine linen and purple.*

...Charm is deceitful and beauty is vain,
but a Woman who fears the lord, shall be
praised.
{Proverbs 31:10,12, & 30}

#

THE SALT AND FLOWER OF THE EARTH

Black women, like all women, look to beauty in a narcissistic container of shampoo, some vesicle of perfume or a bottle of salient lotion to charm, some fragrance that says, "I'm lovely." "I am beautiful." Dark and lovely is not out there somewhere in the dark but evolving from inside our inner light. I am not criticizing cosmetics or beautifiers or the many wonderful women who sought after hope or improvement from a bottle. Beauty enhancements and pretty clothes are important to women and their natural self-expression and need to flower. I am not suggesting dreadlocks to perms curls, African outfits to Italian cuts, or tribal dress codes to business wear. African eccentrics or whatever else you choose in fashion, or believe in, should be "your thing," your way, in your time, your space and obviously by your means and discretion; all that should fall perfectly in place for you. However, if you favor to wear African dress one should do everything possible to expand and blossom self-esteem—self-worth, self-embrace. Loving yourself is what's quintessentially important here. Love the

divine and kind God in you and by this the
floods of dark and lovely will emerge.

There are unknown possibilities of power
dormant and awaiting every woman's
subconscious DNA or blood-print files. They
are filled with bursting anticipation, waiting
to be the real you. In her are thousands of
years of genetic proof of this hidden
magnificence.

> *Let the husband render to his wife the*
> *Affection due her, and likewise also the*
> *wife to Her husband.*
> *{1 Corinthians 7:3}*

How does one help to unlock the many years of restricted power and potentials?

Remember the story of Sinbad, the
romantic thief of Bagdad? -Not the comedian.
Sinbad was a Robin Hood type that robbed from
the rich to support the poor. He was
challenged to conquer all odds and obstacles
to retrieve the sacred blue rose to free his
lady-fair from the unconscious plight of evil.
He bargained his own life because he knew
there would be no real existence without her
companion and love--his better half of

himself. He conquered all these trials and challenges for the freedom of his love, his woman.

It is by this, like the Aladdin's lamp, lay the key to reviling the genie's power. Romance and love are that genie that will open your bride, betroth and lover's heart. This is the key to the health of families. This is her song, her need for courting and a lifetime of romantic ritual. Just as sports might be an object of high praise, physical triumph, testosterone outlet and joy for some men, romance is equally an important part of the "love seed" for women. Just as men scream at the TV quarterback as if "his team" heard him thus the same with Bridezilla programs when her "perfect day" is falling apart—they are just as or equally passionate.

She copes just fine with "reality." But it is love and romance that she holds to high standards. This is her idea of a good sports game. Oh, she understands long hours and hard work but that never prioritizes family time— even if church is that only time together.

Lovers must ritualize your dedication (plan), commitment and love to this "romantic reality." It needs events. It is this thing that captures the conscience of the queen and thereby the health of the family— "If momma is happy, everybody…" Why do you think the movie industry created the genre "chick movies," "steamy romance novels," OWN network and "WE Channels" (women's entertainment)? They all cater to the muse clues women are charmed by—does ESPN do anything less for men? Nope. This is her intrinsic reality—at least for most women anyway.

It does one (man) well to adhere, entertain and accept these behavior needs. By these cues, his home will be happier, and he'll live a lot longer--really.

She is always, no matter how tough or strong, appreciates some damsel in distress assistance—no pitied love but a hand of chivalry is nice. Modern day distress can be almost anything. It is not necessarily a damsel who is rope-tied to a train track by some dastardly villain. With an oncoming locomotive in the distance ensuing her, hero, "Mr. Buck" dashes to her rescue might be cute for a silent movie plot but not during these dog days and rough times. The train track tragedy doesn't quite compare. Now-a-day our damsels need chivalry assistance with financial pitfalls, scandal, social decadence, spiritual deprival's, emotional breakdowns, psychological warfare, AIDS phobia, single parenting, marriage desertion and weight gain all qualify modern "distress." She may need a willing hand in these areas. Life itself is often her "dastardly villain."

Most adult Brown women have learned how to handle life—they are forced too. Oh, she can make it do what it do. However, a "Sistah" might need a Carthaginian "black warrior knight's" (Hannibal) to help fight the woeful everyday battles with such little "love fuel" out there. That's a friend or someone to brighten her world with encouragement, hope, and leadership when asked for, however with mutual faith, friend security and celebrated happiness with a strong but loving hand. This simply means the couple, two of you, working and deciding things together as one. To her, love from brother prince, is the key to her coping with the frightening unknowns of the world and the wolves therein. Oh again, "Onyxi-locks" (or Goldilocks) is very strong and can handle those "life wolves" but a little help from her friends wouldn't hurt.

She has powerful Wonder Woman like emotions, but that great power can be a detriment where the good friend (a man; a romantic friend) comes in to upset, reset and refocus her expectations with nonsense testosterone OCD know-how. She is better equipped to master and cope than most men but

if your flanging love tends to deregulate, get
rocky, with comings and goings of affairs,
this could be her kryptonite of uncertainty.
Sturdy as she goes is the emotional code for
this Amazon power.

So, who is brother prince?

He's the man, who is polite, honest, not
necessarily Mr. Over-Ambitious-Gonna Conquer
the world type guy but necessarily Mr. Hard
Worker, i.e., a job, God fearing, kind,
children loving, warm smiles, nice clothes
that feel good and tender kisses, fragrant,
soft touches, other than sex, and Mr.
Compassionate—all that equals the dashing hero
for her. The brown Robin-Hood can be short,
tall, fat, skinny, muscular, not rich, not
poor all those things are important, but they
are never as important as being a committed
and "for-real" man--just a man. Most women are
NOT entertained by silliness, the 3 Stooges
and Bullshit will dry her up fast. But a Papa
bear that's always there, like a strong oak,
gets her flowing. He needs to be a willing
warrior for love who laughs and expresses his
affection and feelings for family. He is a man
who understands that women, not unlike men,
ideally look for tender perfection in a mate.

You know: the perfect build, easy to look at (eye candy), nice butt and normal to bourgie educated backgrounds and "big feet." Of course, no one is perfect, and that mate MUST have that much wisdom. **However**, Mr. and Mrs. Brotha'/Sistah is perfect when they are wisely understanding, a genuine listener, a positive supporter, and a nurturer of "love seeds" (sweet or kind compliments).

We are most perfect when we pot and fertilize one spouse (our flower) at a time faithfully—monogamously and with fidelity. It is these things, behaviors, which make us "ideal" soul mates. When the brother prince is willing to help the woman feel like a brown diamond by mining deep into her heart for dormant treasures, handled delicately like a vault curator, it is in this precious place brother prince will find lasting gems of the rarest kind--"real love" as well as true love.

#

LOVE CHECK LIST:

Think these bulleted questions through and mediate upon them. Your family and you depend upon them for life improvement. Do not make anyone responsible for your answers but YOU.

- How do I sustain my family's love base ("Love fuel," "Love-seeds") reaching-out to them?

- Why haven't I loved myself all along before now?

- How do I know when I am not being my own best friend?

- Is this lack of love in my family karma, some ridiculous cosmic penalty for sin or evil?

- Since Africans are the original people could this be some {"Adamu and Eva (Usika)"} i.e., Adam & Eve unforgotten DNA thing, some un-forgiven thing held over by gods? A begrudging God? Or some forgiving but dues collecting god?

- What is self-hate? What pisses me off so when I fight and fuss?

- Should I blame "our White founding fathers and mothers" and their past for current issues among Browns?

- Just what does make Brown women and men beautiful and attractive?

- What sort of "attitudes" do I find calming and attractive in other races? Can I be that too?

- How tall should I be and thin should you be before I find other friends?

- Am I the leader or boss in *my* home or are *we* the leaders and boss in *our* home?

- Do you respond, "How high?" when I say, "Jump" or do we both have that equal privilege?

Families can have real power and/or real money when I/we support each other just as we've been supporting the world. Brown support is more than a car wash, a lawn cut, a haircut, "doo-dids" or tithing paid. It's contributing economics. If I support the world, yet it isn't willing to live next door to me, embrace me, I might want to re-think my misdirected support.

If these above questions make you think, then that's their intent to get you/us to think. I want to provoke a desire to change for the better-good. I hope that we're well on our way to putting away old habits and incorporate new prayers and meditations by staying aware of the world around us, so we'll know what to pray for. It's an entire wayward topic, but God is intelligent if nothing else. Getting to know "it" (Him, Her) is ascertaining its knowledge hence knowing better to direct our prayers. We have the courage to change for respectability and self-esteem unto ourselves, our men, our babies and especially our Brown woman who is the carrier of future blood-prints and love-seeds.

CODA

The Brown woman is a precious thing like every other living thing god has created. We must praise her love for being strong but gentle, powerful, yet compassionate, reprimanding without cruelty, and being the boss without being bossy.

I recognize that Brown women have more power than she thinks or could even imagine, and the fuel of that power is God's grace and man's helpmeet.

She is our flower—our 'blue Aladdin rose'. The blue rose in this case is the Brown man himself, his "inner-good," "decency," monogamy and "nobility" that he must retrieve from her lost self; charged to help her to rediscover and reinvent herself.

Sinbad's blue rose is the symbol of love and faith overcoming all obstacles for his damsel in life-distress. Restoring his love's consciousness back to self-love, back to cornucopia of euphoria, back to self-awareness and inner bliss is our male job. And it starts with a simple smile, a warm hand for assistance, encouraging forgiveness and our approval to "do it" and "go for it," i.e., her dreams. Remember, she is our power base, the object whence life springs and our "Helpmeet."

"And the Lord God said that it is not good that man should be alone; I will make him a help meet for him." Genesis 2:18

She doesn't mind being the "HELP" as long as she FEELS inside the Brown man is ALWAYS meeting her halfway—75% is better yet; feels warmer against her 110% that she will always offer him--provided she chooses you to love.

That is the caveat. Never take that for
granted either. Because she is nice, or dates
you, or speaks to you she might loves you.
When she loves you, heaven and earth won't
stop her will to show you. Sure, women like
lovers but they adore committed *friends* who
love her a lot better.

     With these dedications, it doesn't matter
if the non-complimenting dreadful world around
her calls her: Negro, Niggra, Colored,
African, Afro, Brown, Mulatto, Black
Bourgeoisie or from the Bouquet Race in a
derogatory matter or otherwise. The power of
your noble love will keep her esteem insulated
and in tack with confidence of what she and
her family is—that will be untouchable, Teflon
magnificent, bold & beautiful, dark, and
lovely.

     Our mission, as men, should you choose to
accept it, is to retrieve the confidence of
your adoring Brown woman.

Yes, sure, she is the key to her own self-esteem but you're the support that will help her rise to an all-time level that WILL one day bud the dormant Blood-prints of our first hominid human dynasty where queens and kings will once again emerge. No, this is not for vengeance but natural maturation and the releasing of greatness.

Men, you are not the tree, but you are the trim that manages the germination of reform for her growth. In her are four hundred years of lost growth, she waits to flower in full bloom and splendor. Whenever and whatever that will be? Only God knows. But what we (men) do know, there is beauty and power untapped "because God can do anything but fail." -Rev Dr. Odell Smith, Jr.

Her "love seeds" are in dormancy awaiting the shower of our sun shining kisses to make a difference, Mr. Prince.

today with ONE REAL KISS FROM BROTHER PRINCE
will reset our Bouquet Race forward to course.
At least, that is my fasting prayer.

The Beginning

Next is series #3

Would you let your ego die for me?

(Now is the time for the harvest of families...)

Thank you, Google, for your endless sources,
and thank you audience for reading

NOTES

www.ingramcontent.com/pod-product-compliance
Lightning Source LLC
Chambersburg PA
CBHW031059250726
48655CB00004B/1501